AF255957

PRIDE & REFUSE

PRIDE & REFUSE

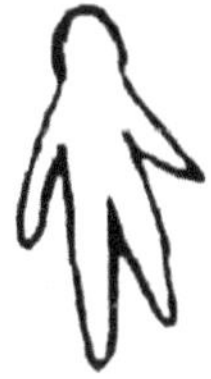

A Safe Little World Monograph
by Andrew Killick

shadow *press*

Pride & Refuse (Special Edition) (SLWM4S)
Published by Shadow Press
New Zealand
www.shadowpress.co.nz

ISBN 978-0-9951189-7-3

Design and typesetting: Andrew Killick

Title typeface: Museo Slab designed by Jos Buivenga
Body typeface: Skolar 10.5/15 designed by David Březina

July 2022

Judge of all things, imbecile worm of the earth;
depositary of truth, a sink of uncertainty and error;
the pride and refuse of the universe.

- Blaise Pascal, *Pensées*

Prologue

there's a quote that always nags around in the back of my head.
i can't shake it. it's creatively compelling. when i first read it,
intermittently staring up at a clear blue sky and what i was reading
as i lay on a recliner in the backyard, i wrote it down in my notebook.
i've had other notebooks since but i get anxious if i don't know
where that notebook is – mainly because i worry about misplacing
the exact wording of the quote.

the quote comes from pascal's *pensées* (VII:434). pascal was one of
the world's great thinkers – a genius of science, but also an astute
observer of the condition of humanity. when he died in 1662 he left
behind an unfinished work, in notebook form. *pensées* (french for
'thoughts') is a collection of notes that he jotted down about life, the
universe and everything.

the quote ('my' quote) is his definition of humankind:

'Judge of all things, imbecile worm of the earth; depositary of
truth, a sink of uncertainty and error; the pride and refuse of the
universe.'

this captures the massive paradox, the tension, in what it is to be
human.

- Blog excerpt (170710)

—

Instructions for looking: Turn your head on its side.
(Or turn the book.)

Part One:
Pride & Refuse

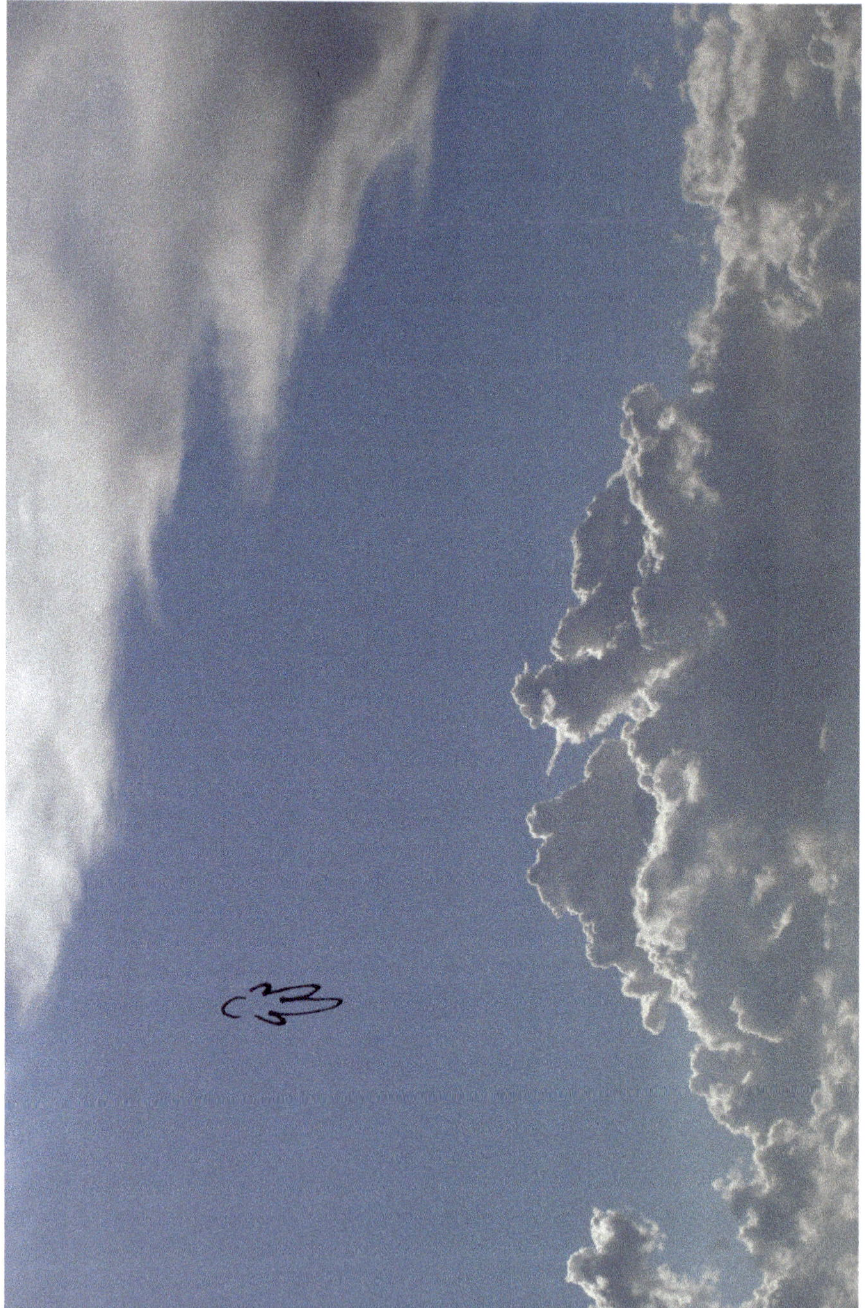

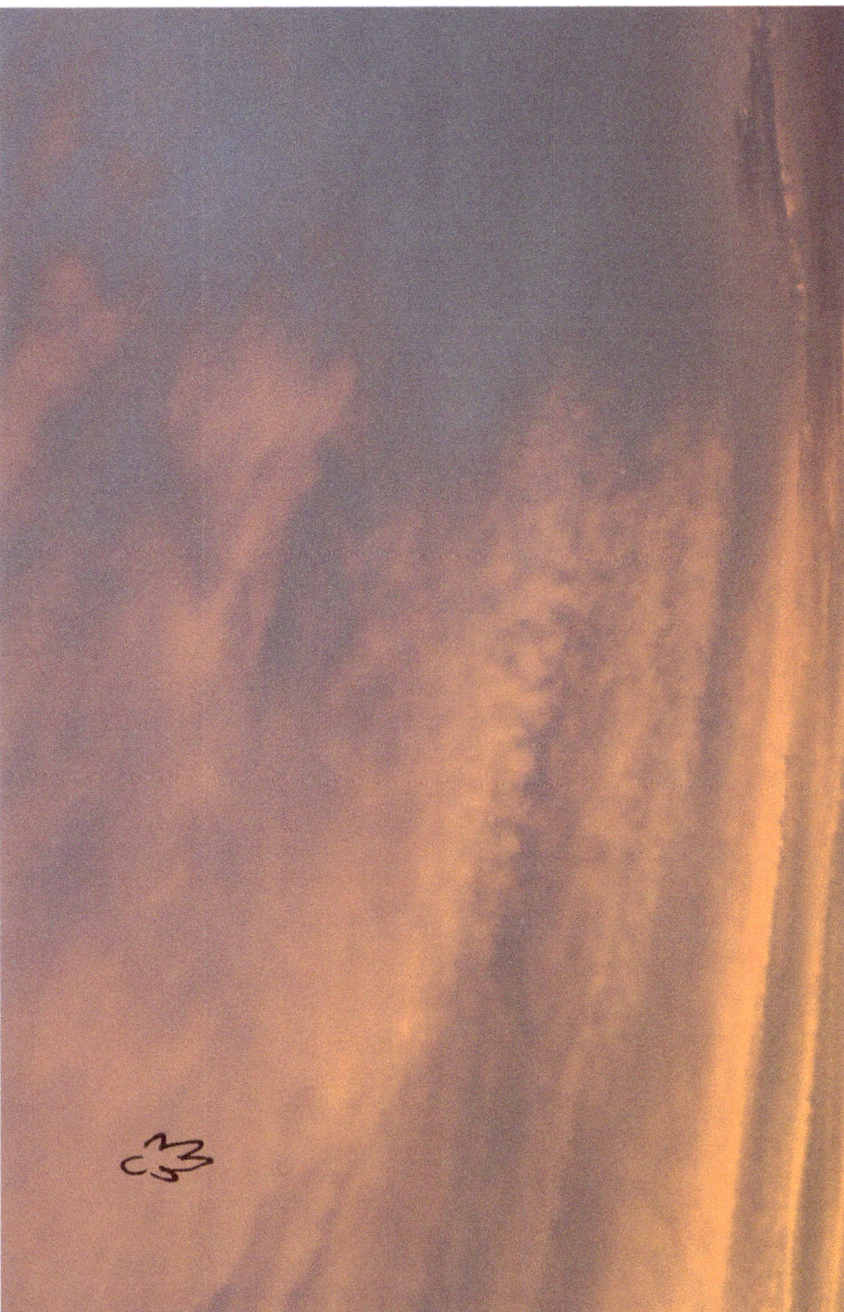

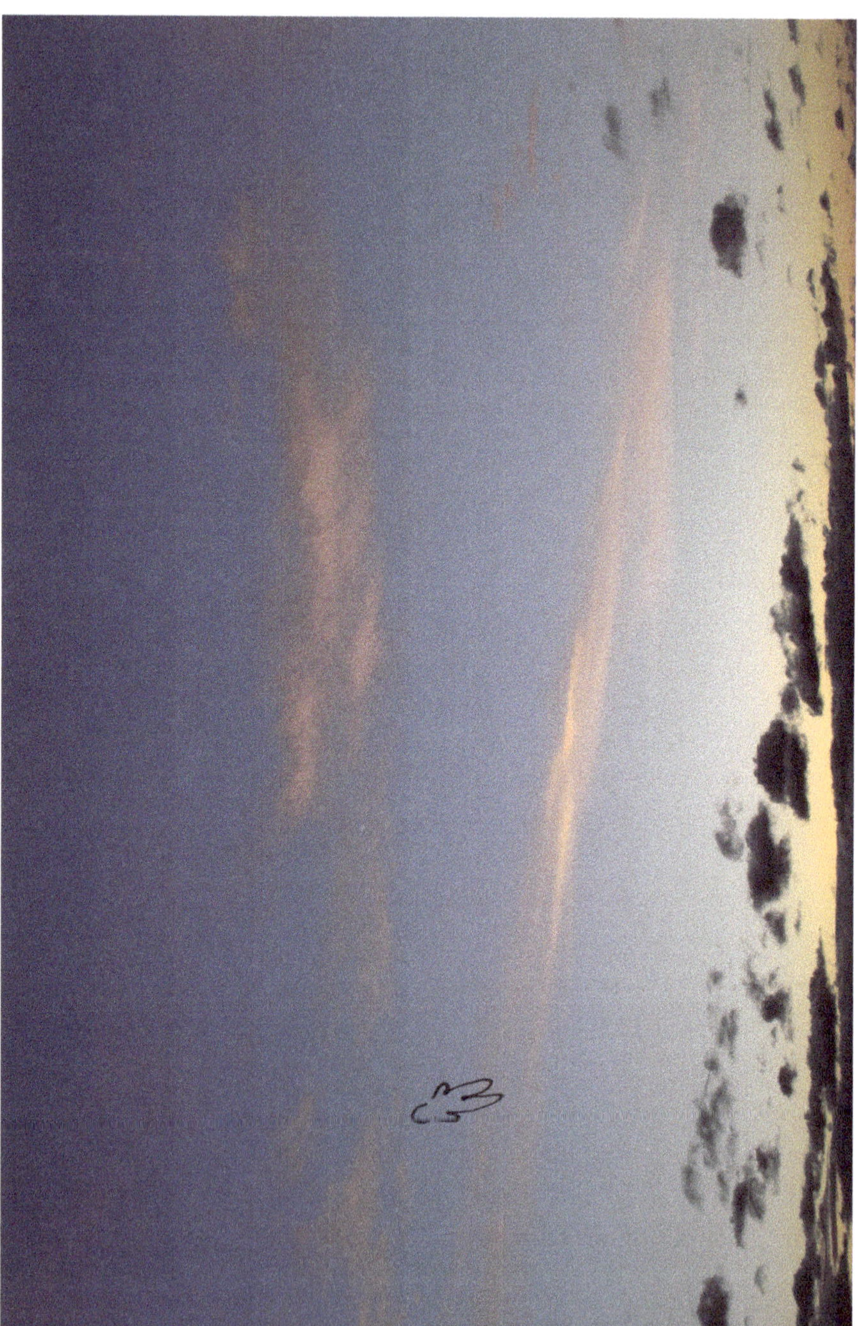

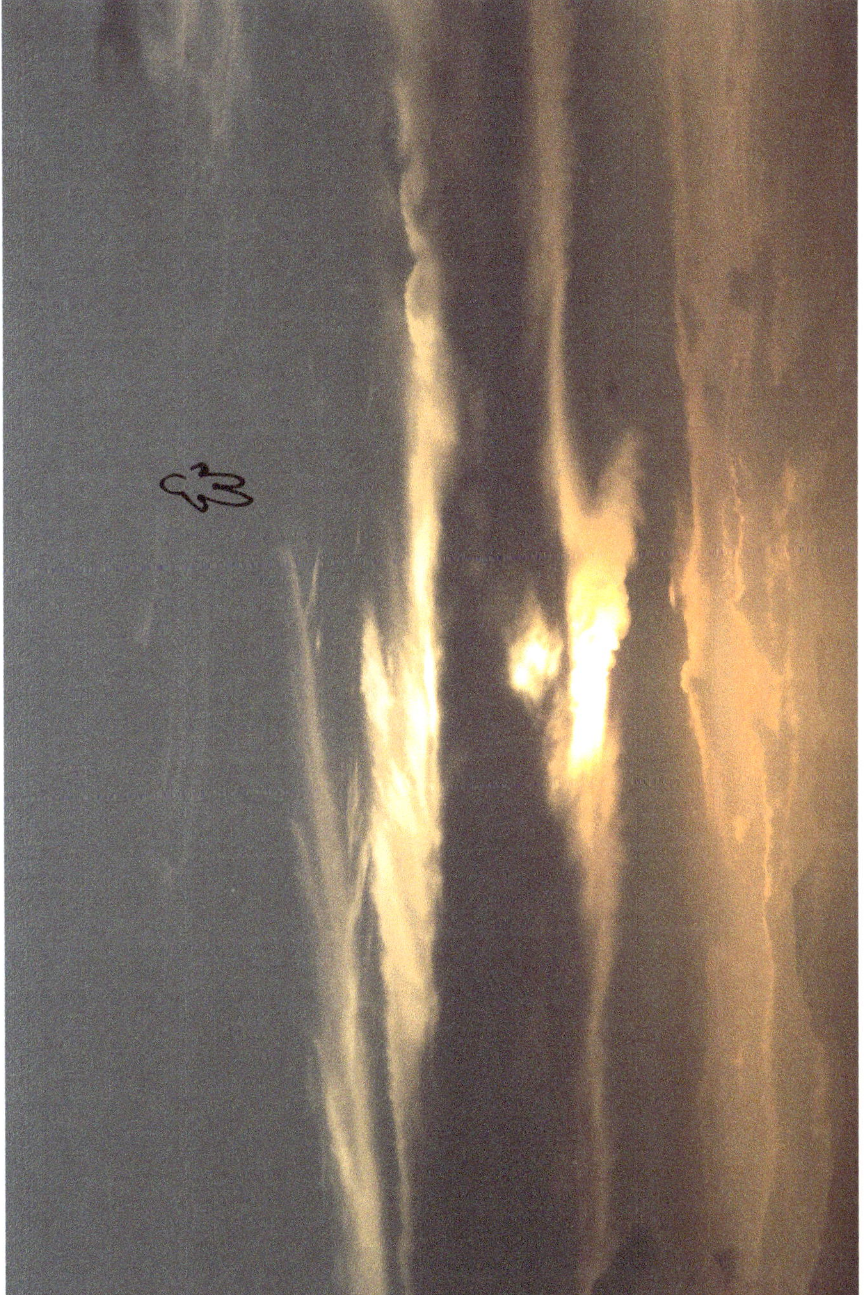

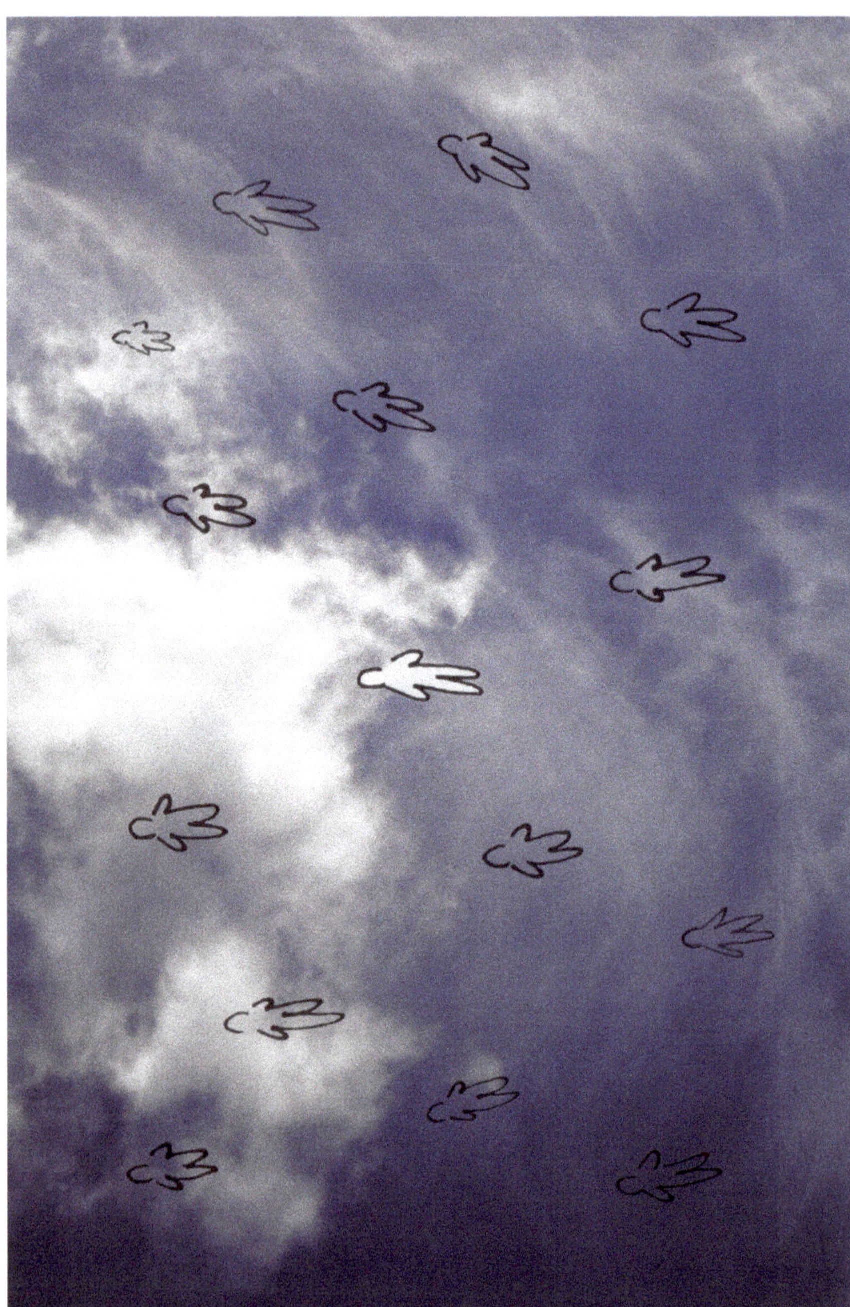

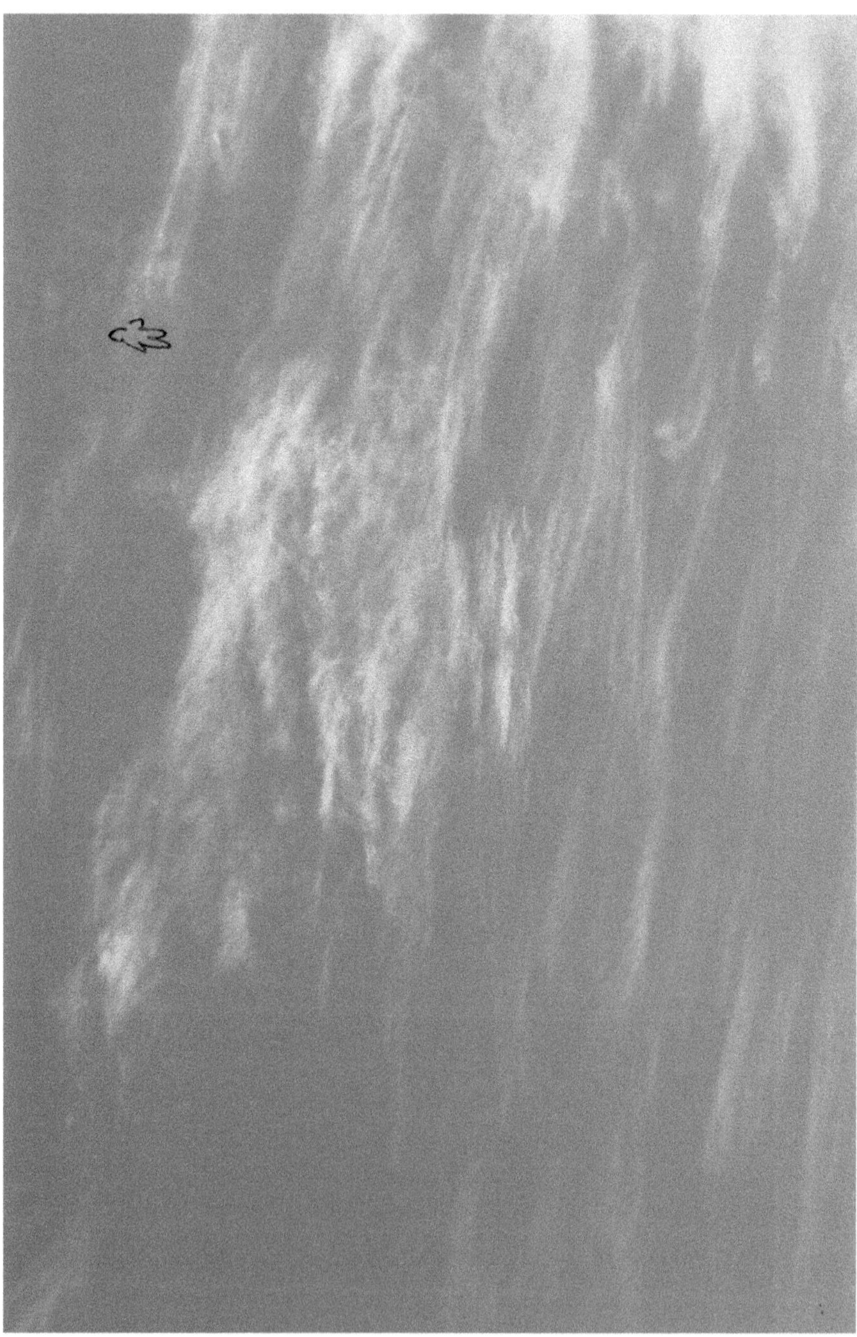

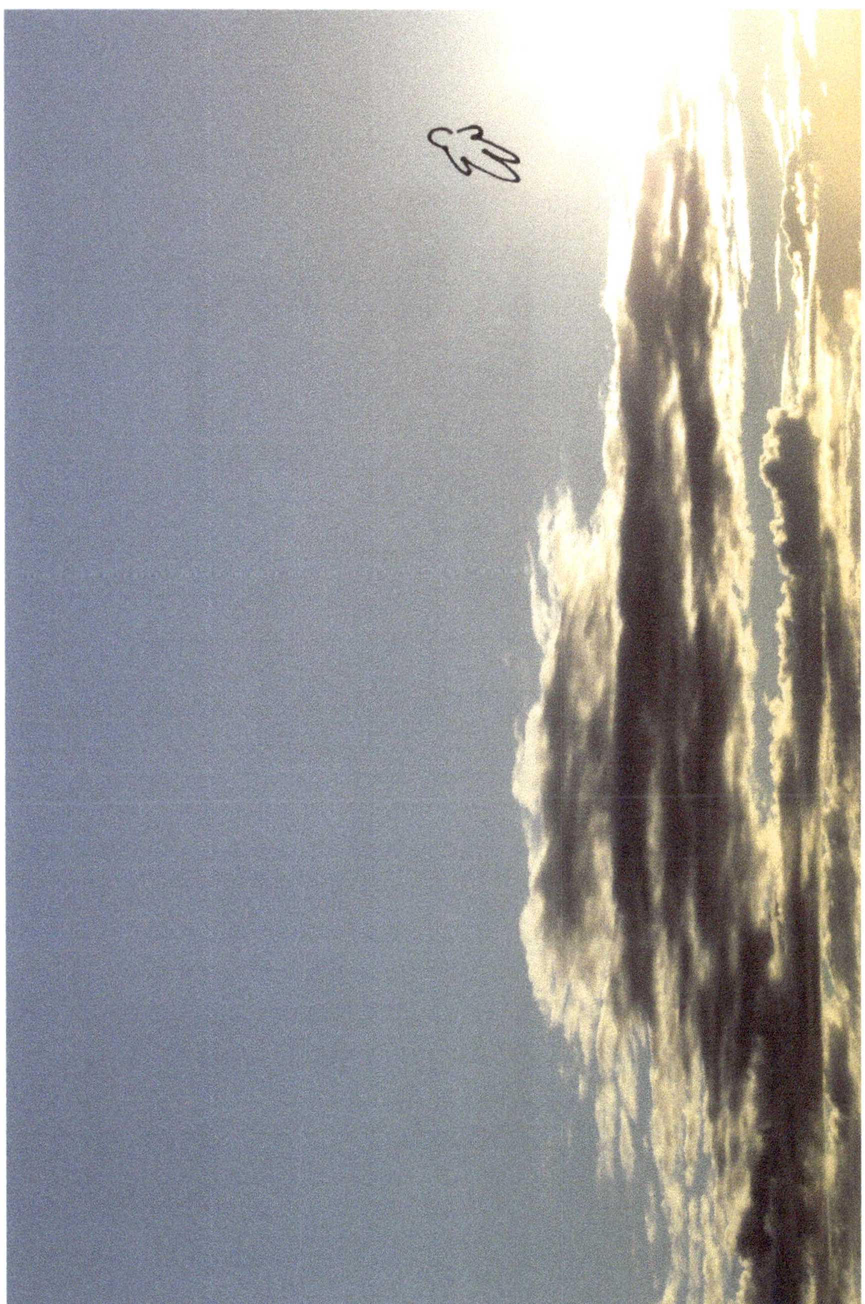

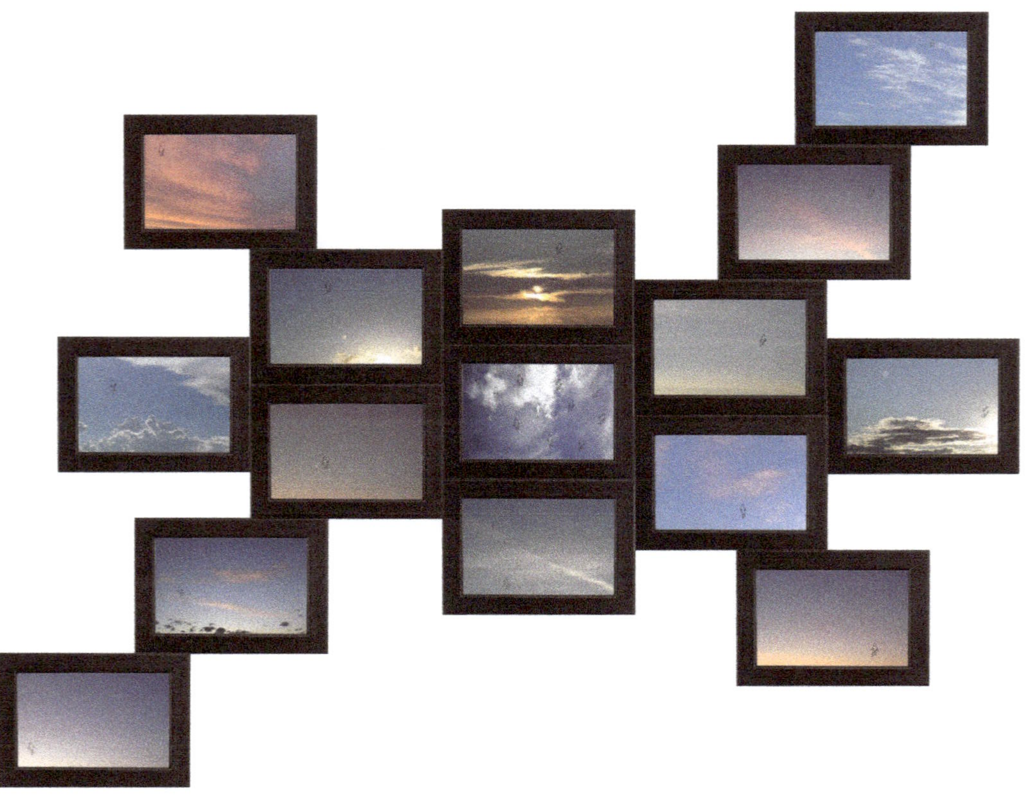

Pride & Refuse – exhibition layout schema.

Part Two:
Rising/Falling

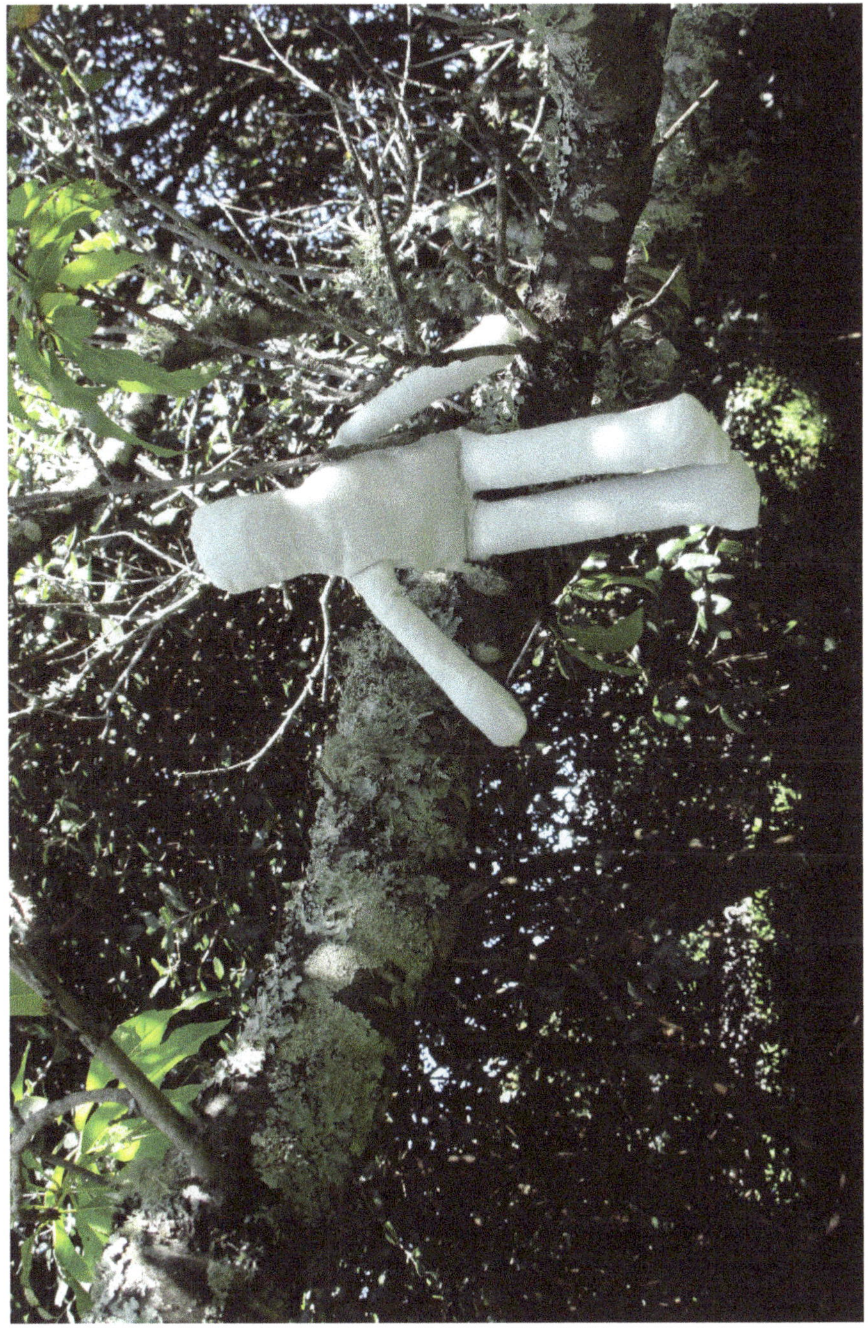

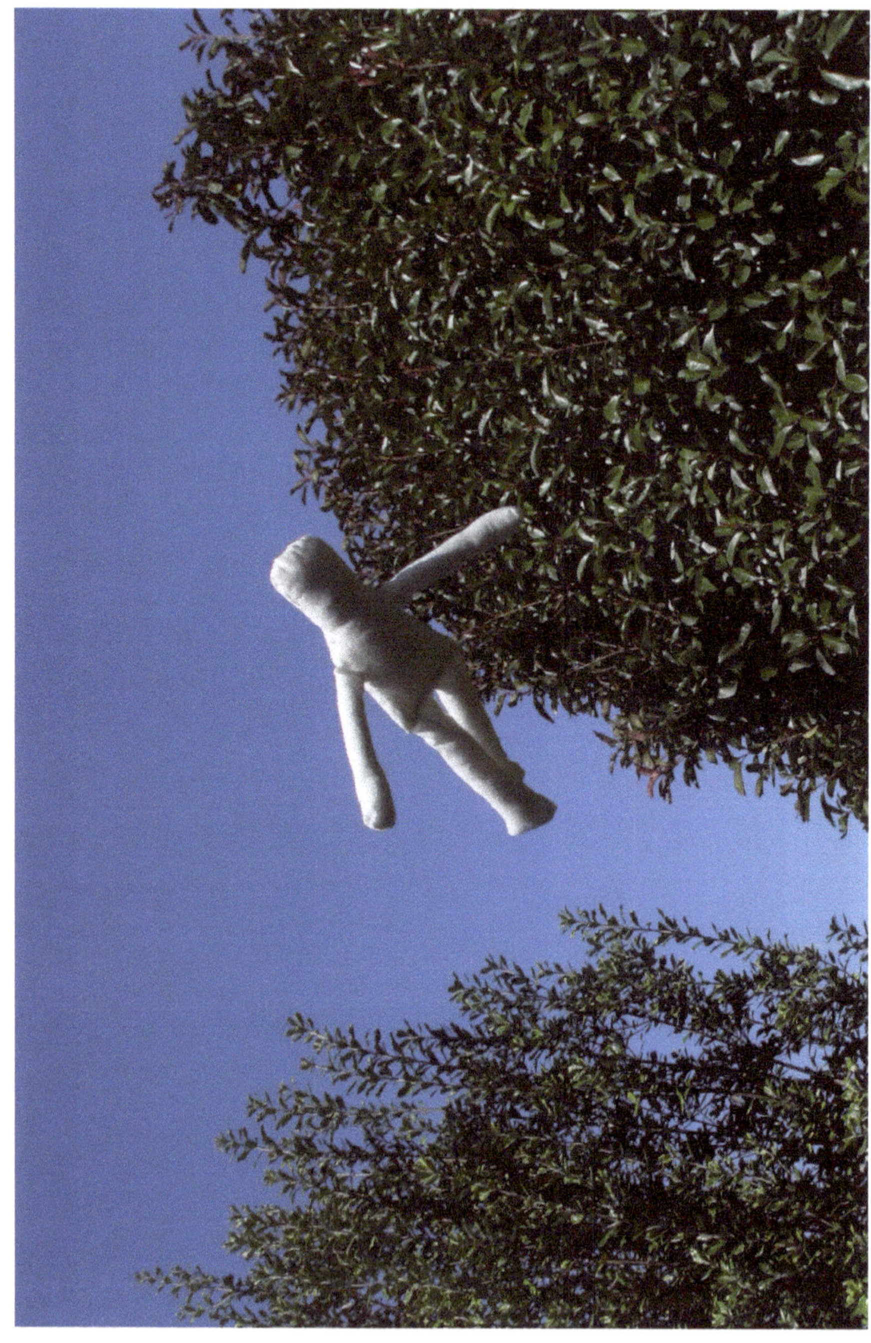

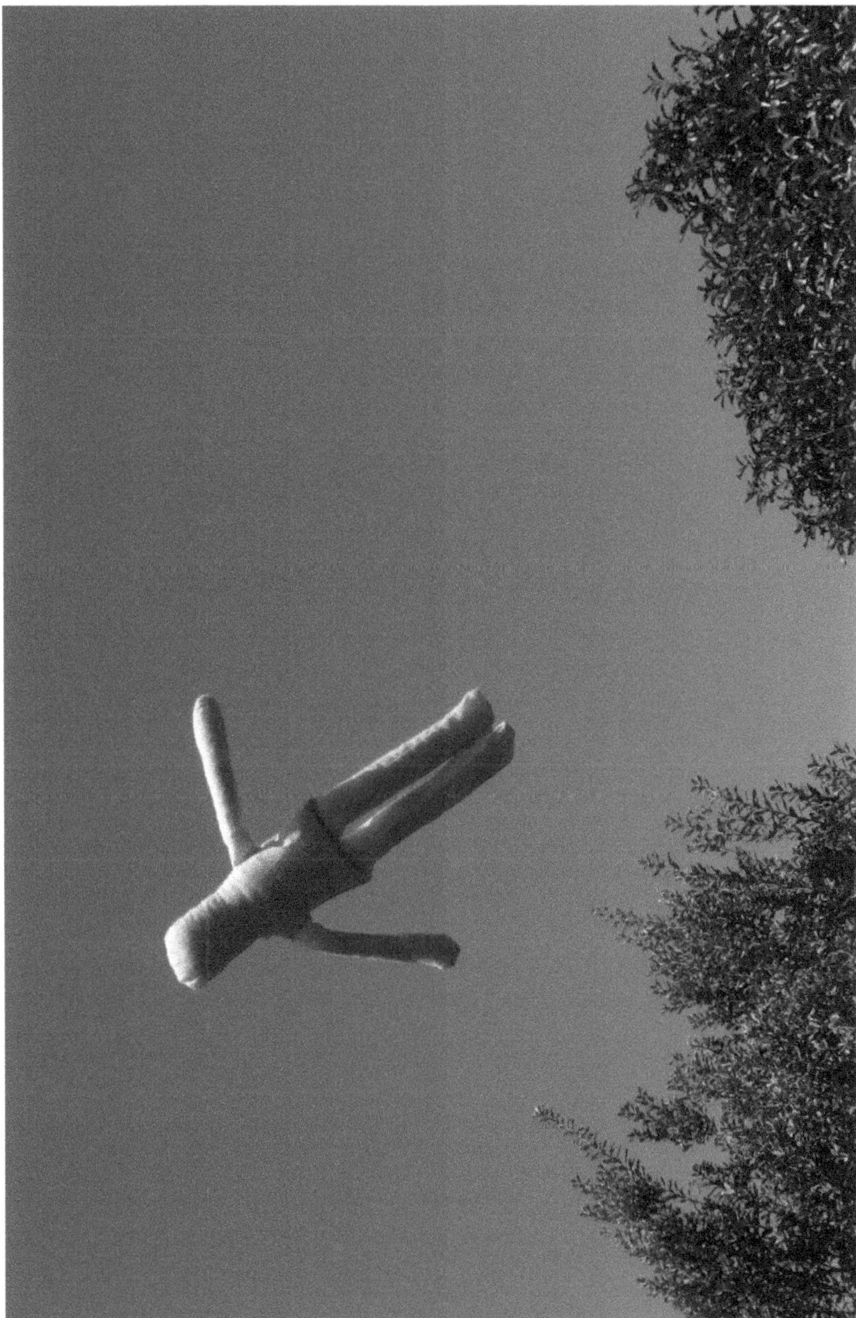

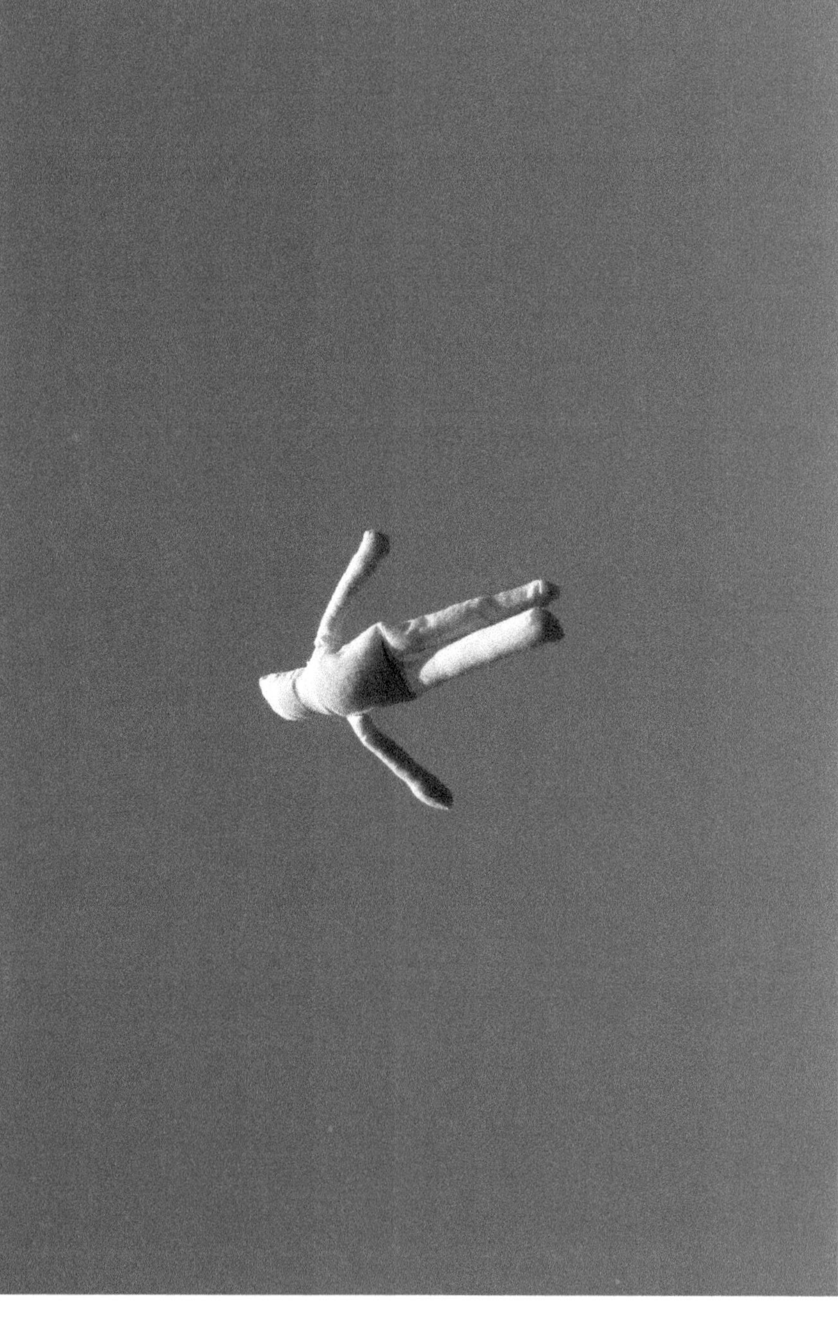

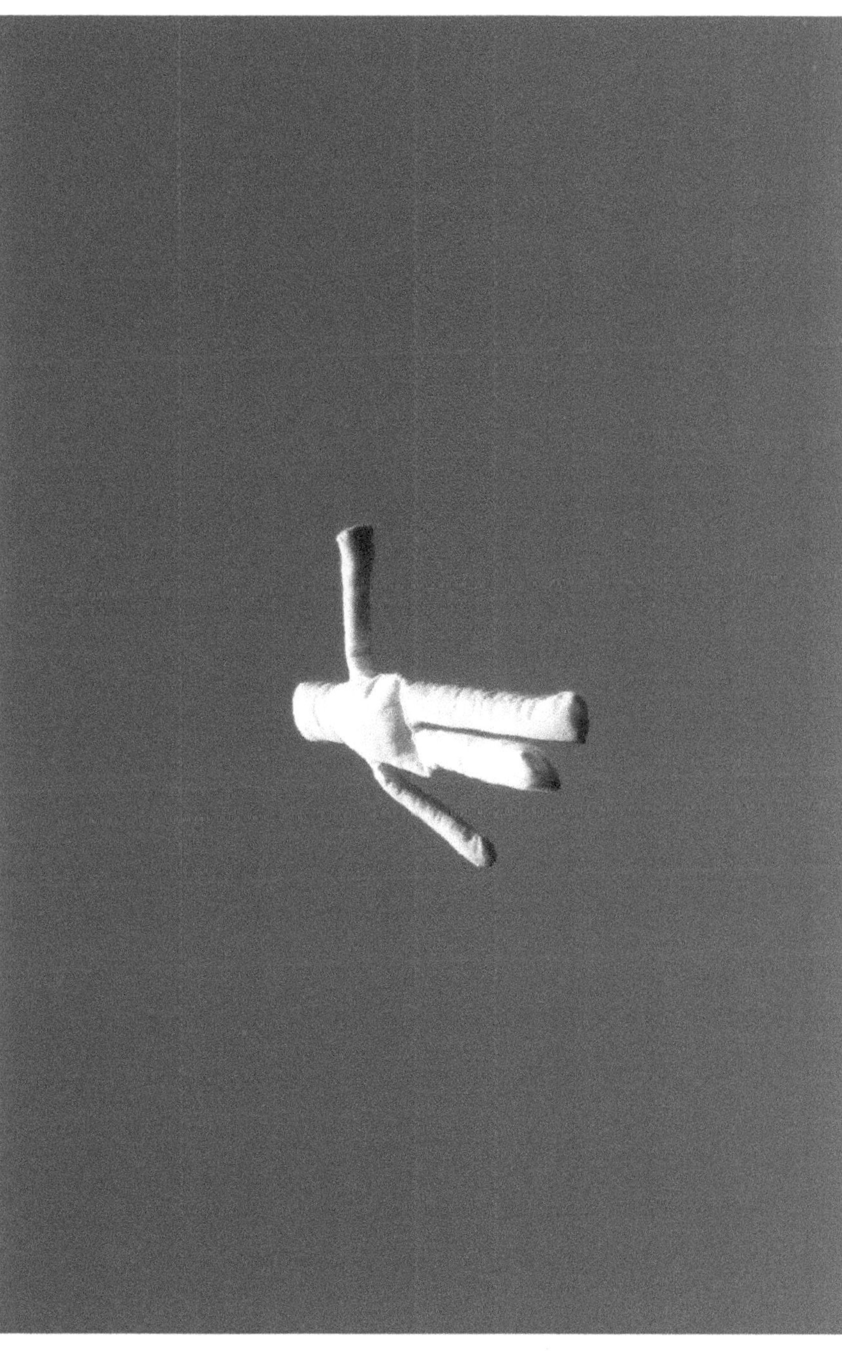

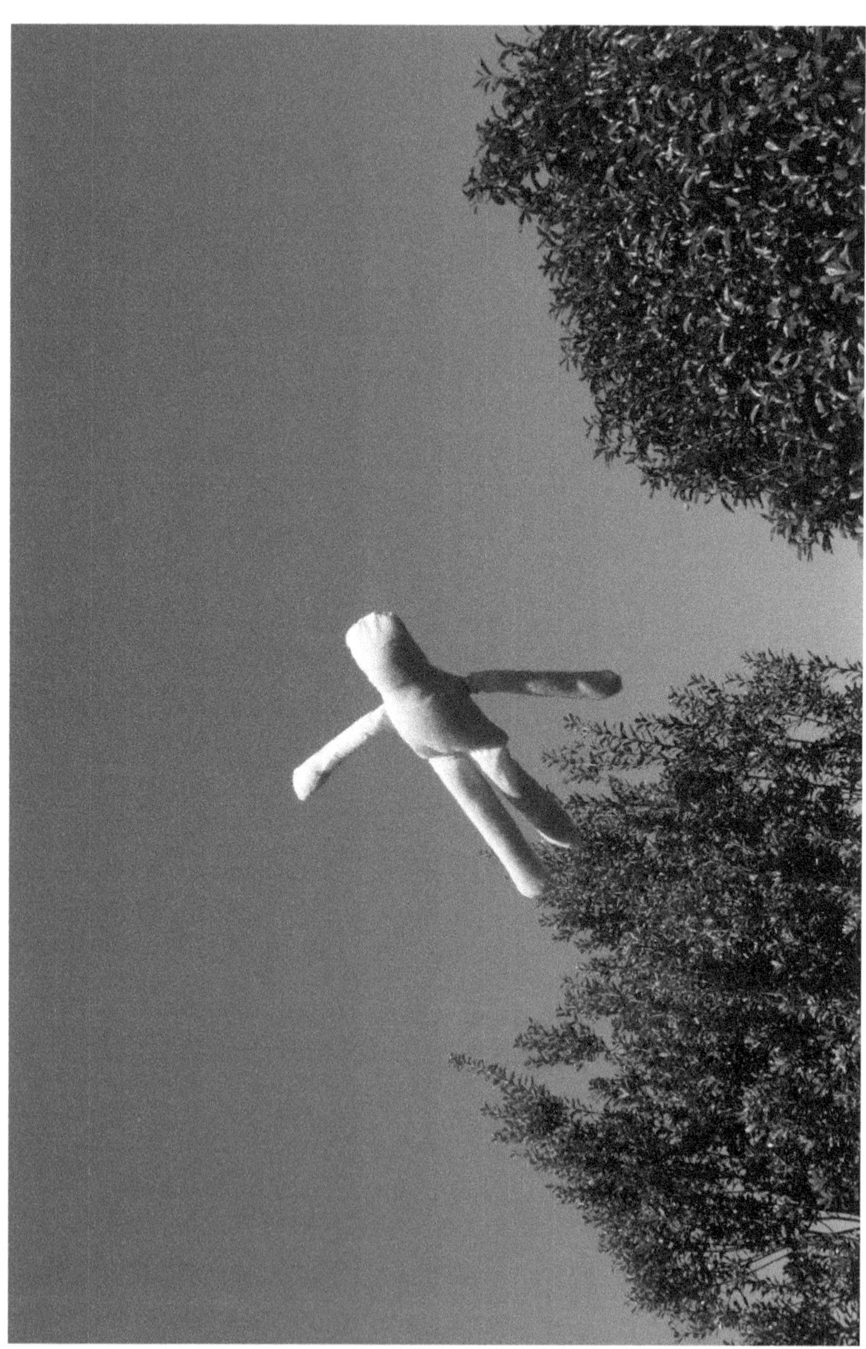

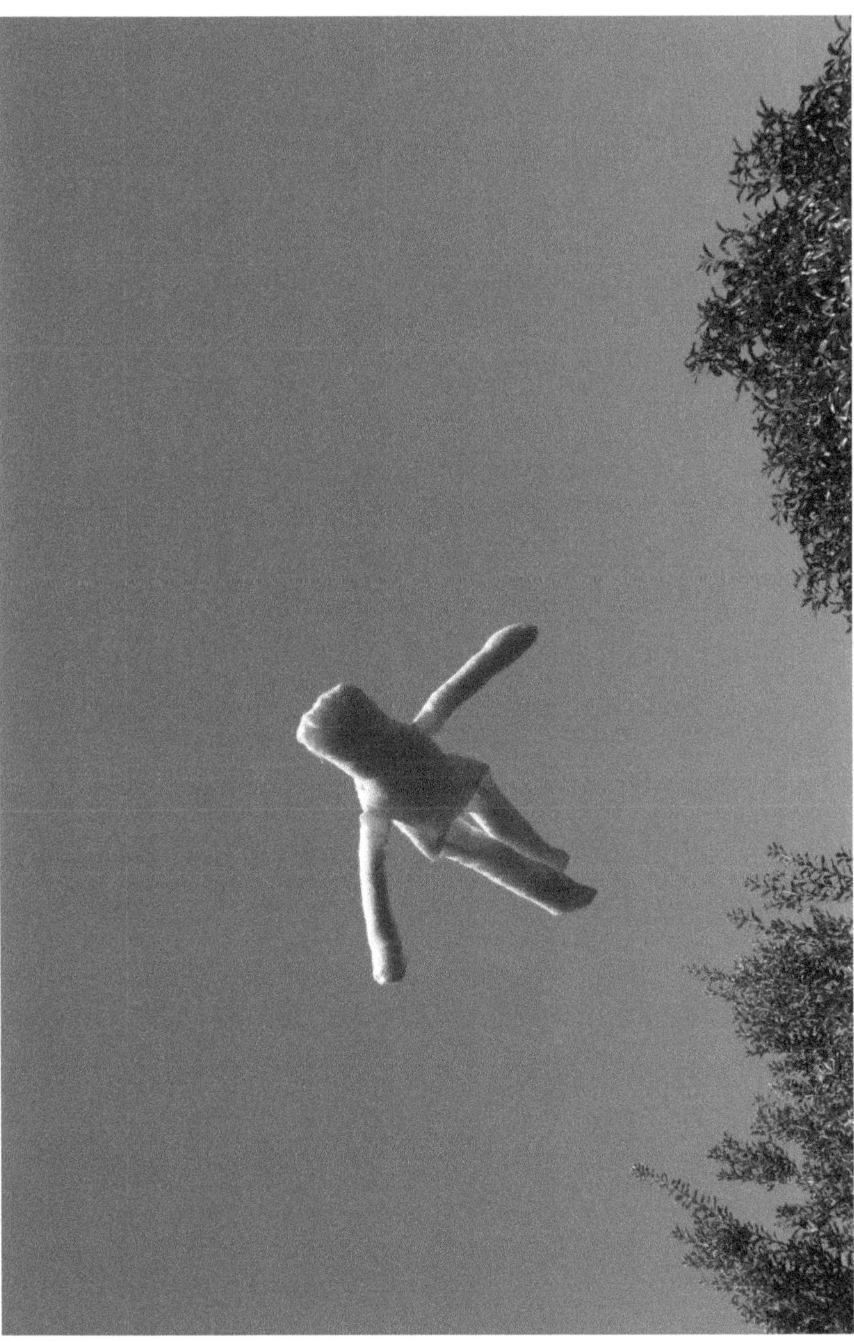

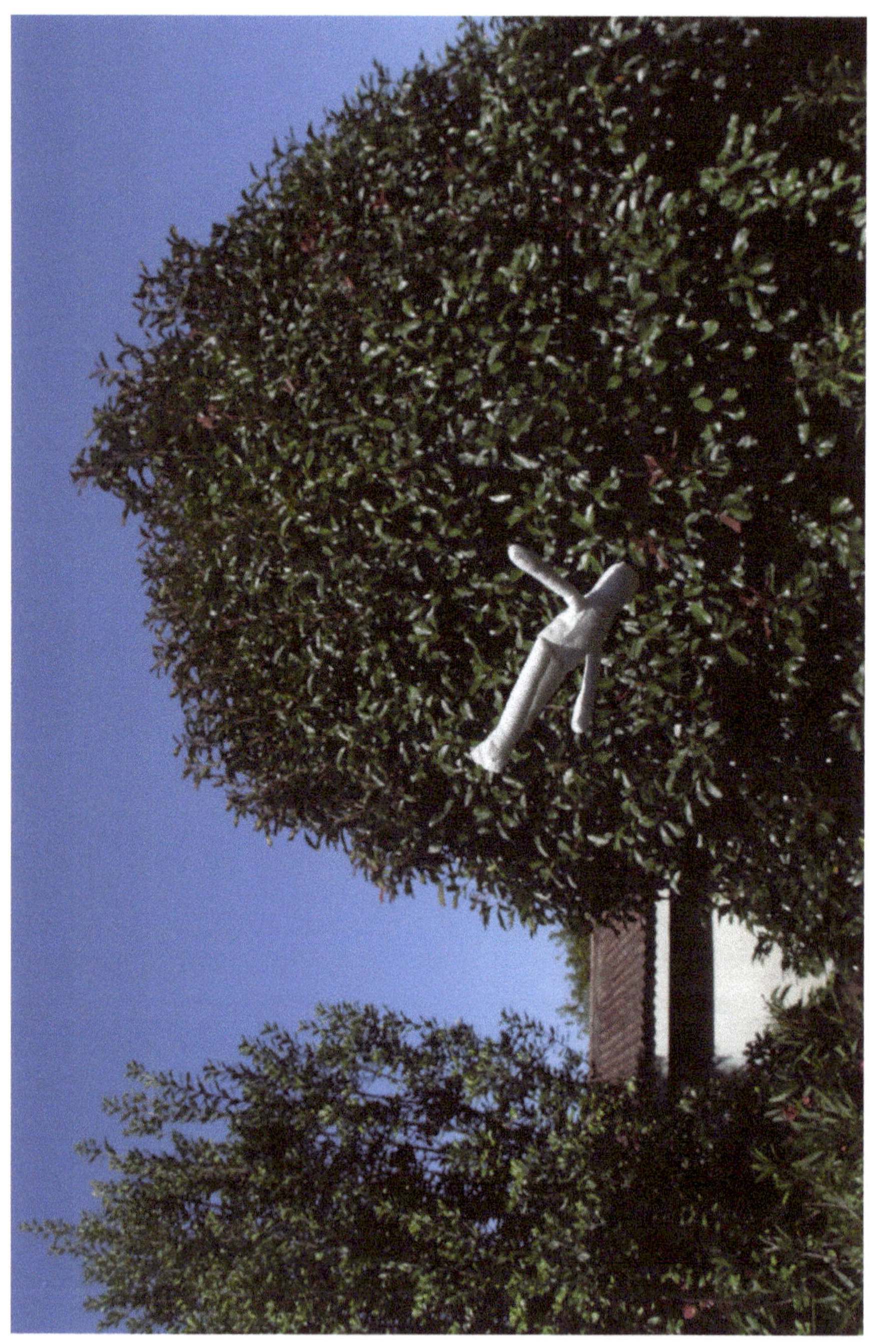

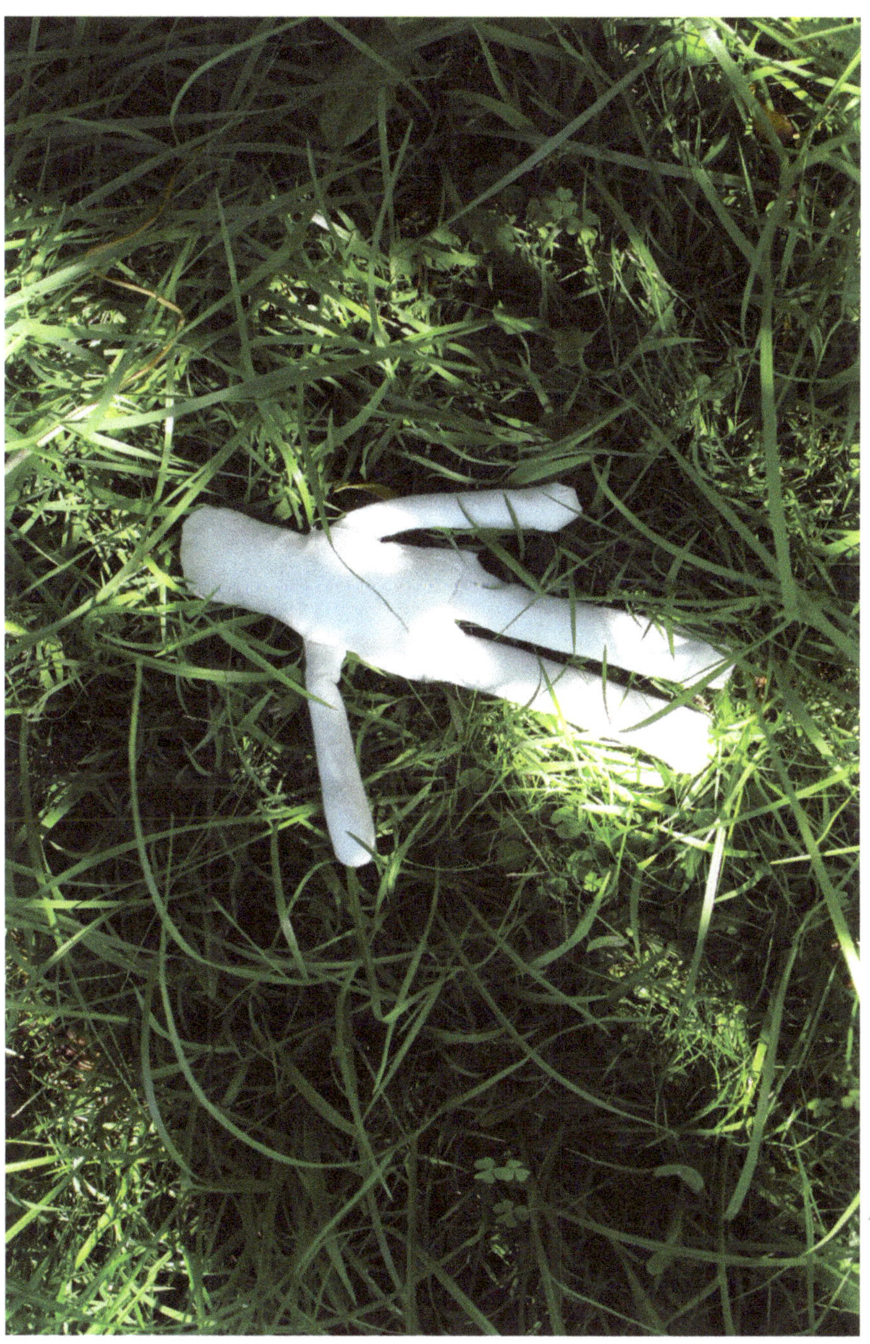

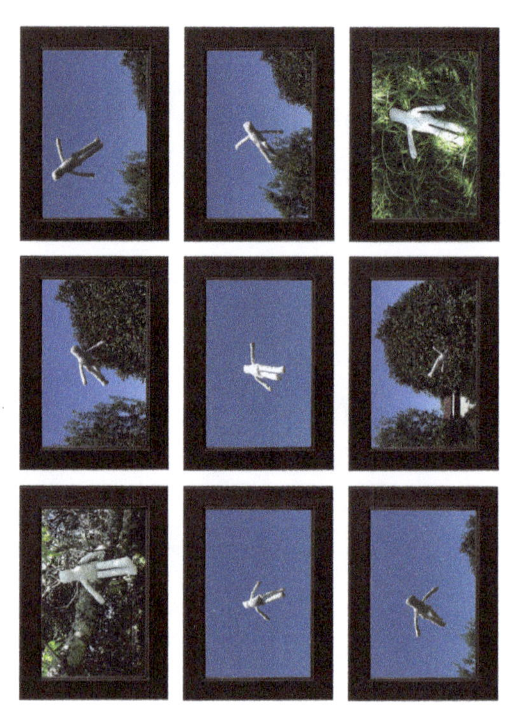

Rising/Falling – exhibition layout schema.

Part Three:
Documentary

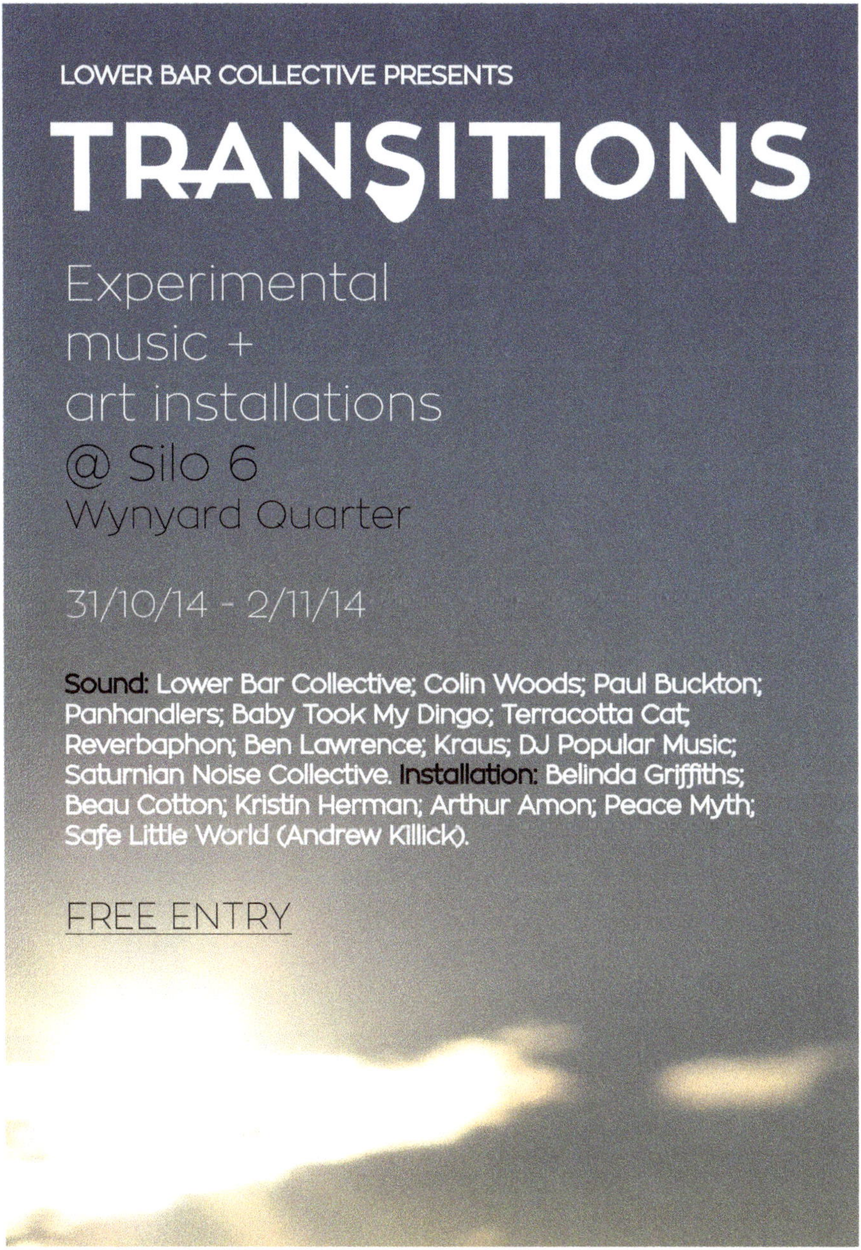

Promotional poster for the Lower Bar Collective curated event in which the Pride & Refuse installation appeared.

—

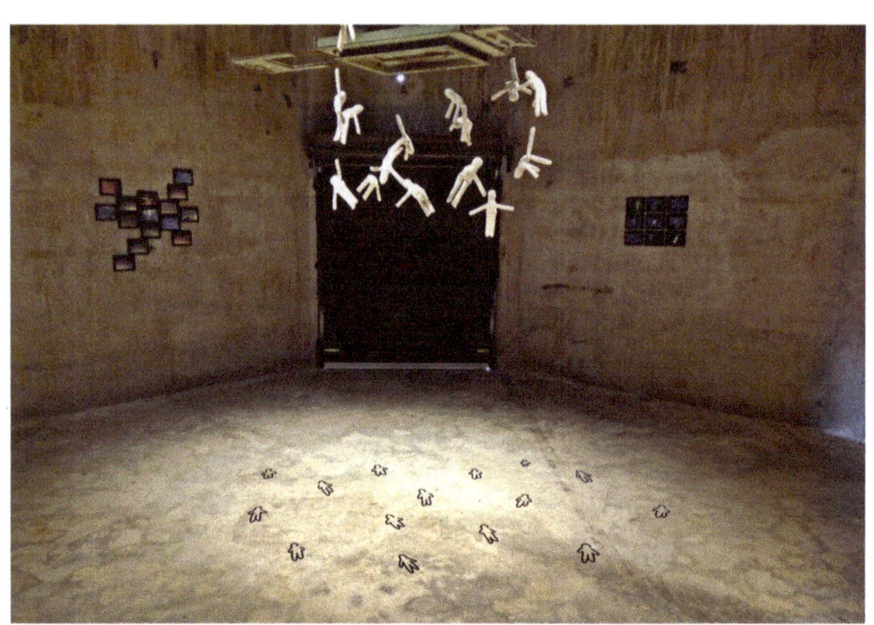

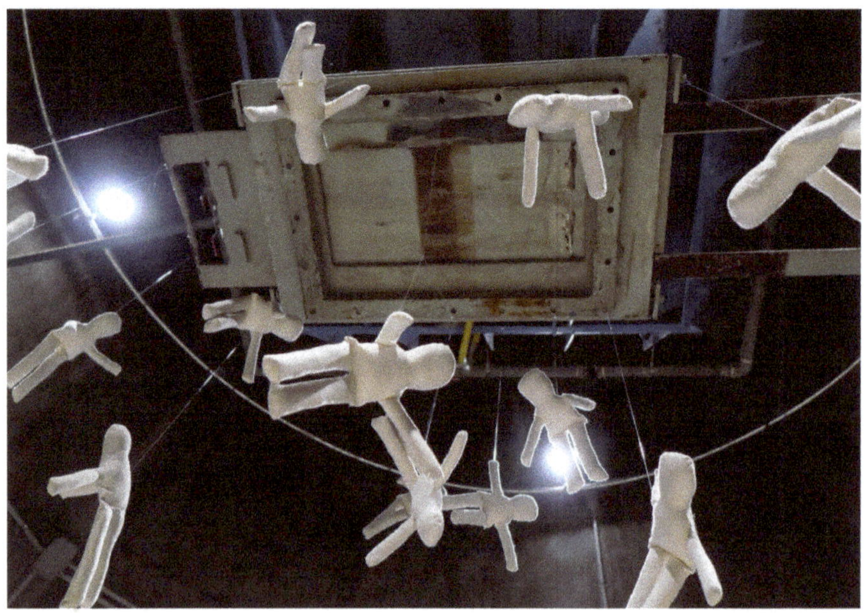

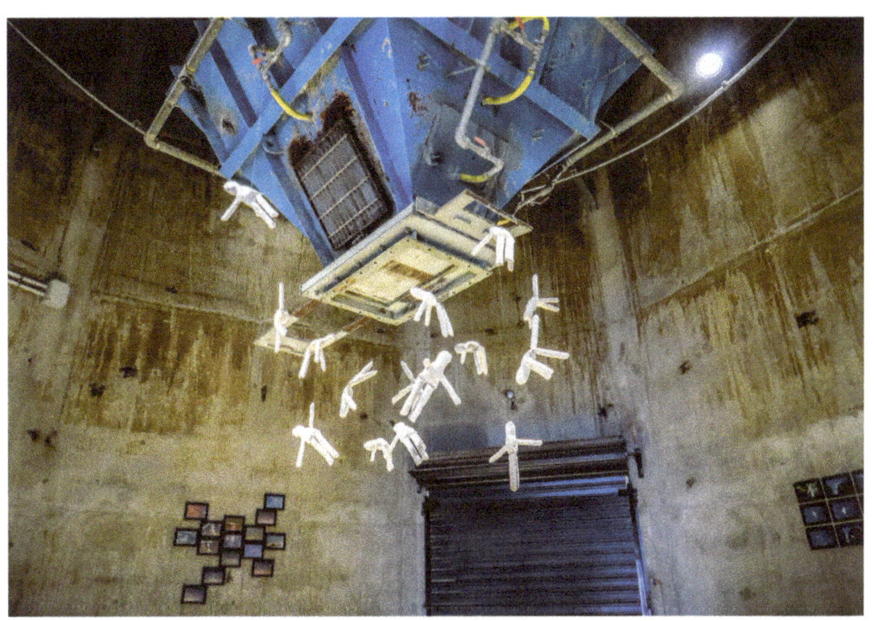

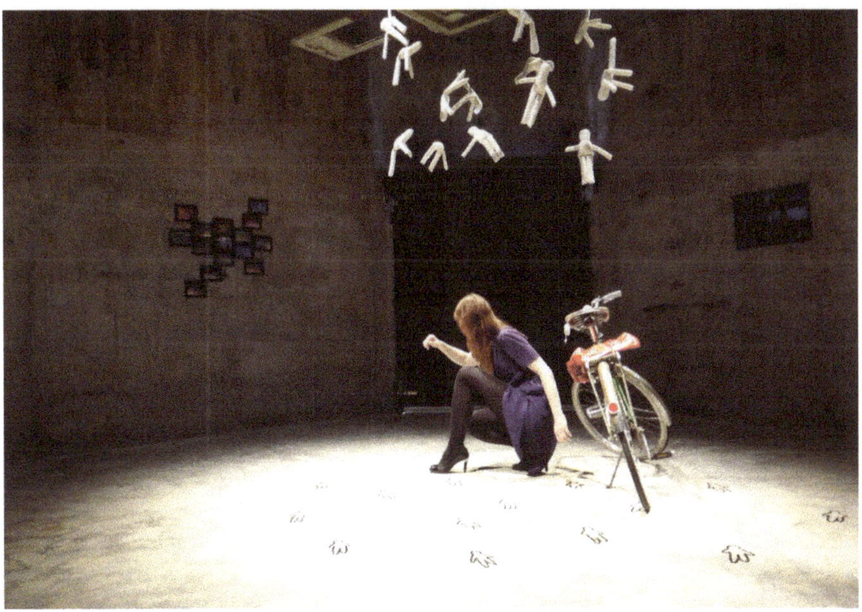

Installation view, Transitions, Silo 6. Bottom right: dance artist Georgie Goater interacts with the installation during a performance with Kristian Larsen.
Images, left to right, by Paul Buckton (1&4) and Dave Simpson Photography (2&3).

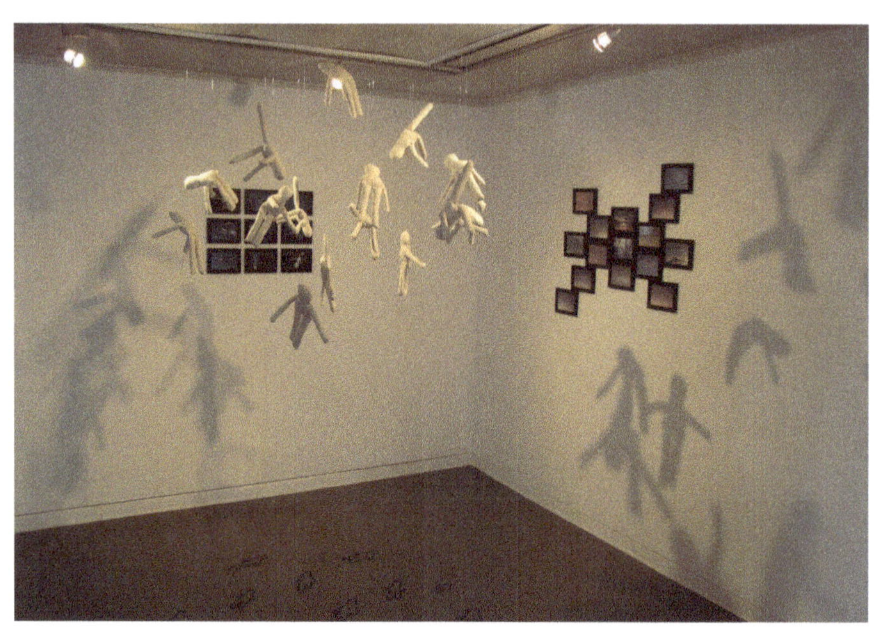

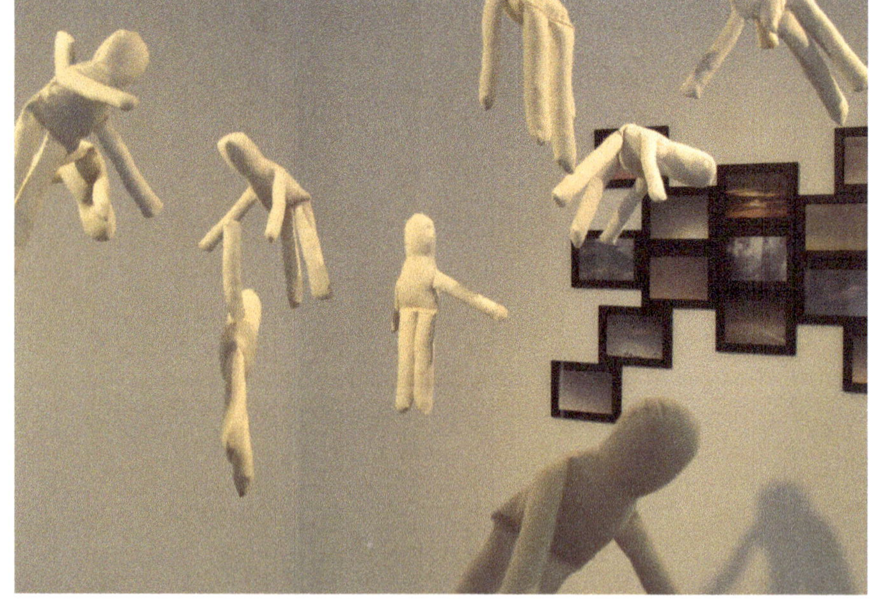

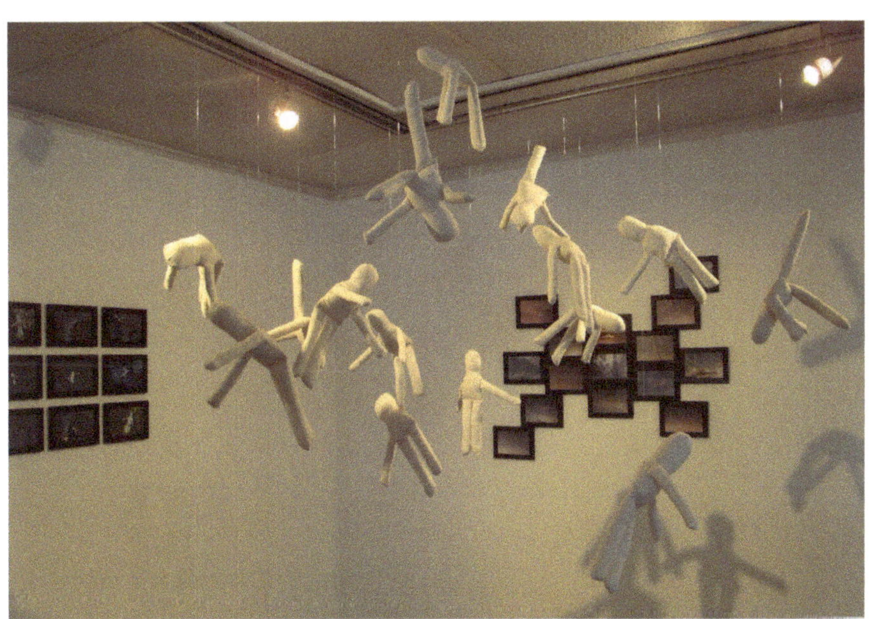

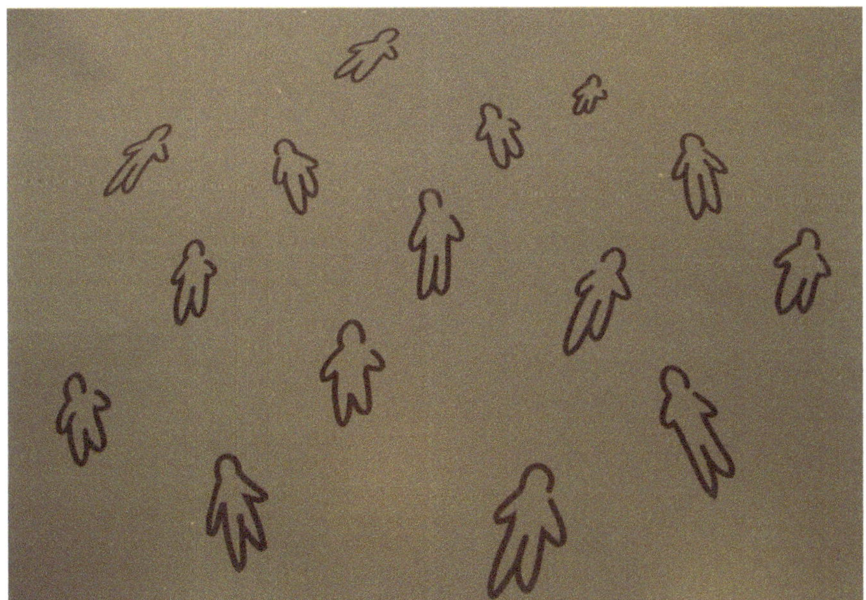

Installation view, Zeus Gallery.

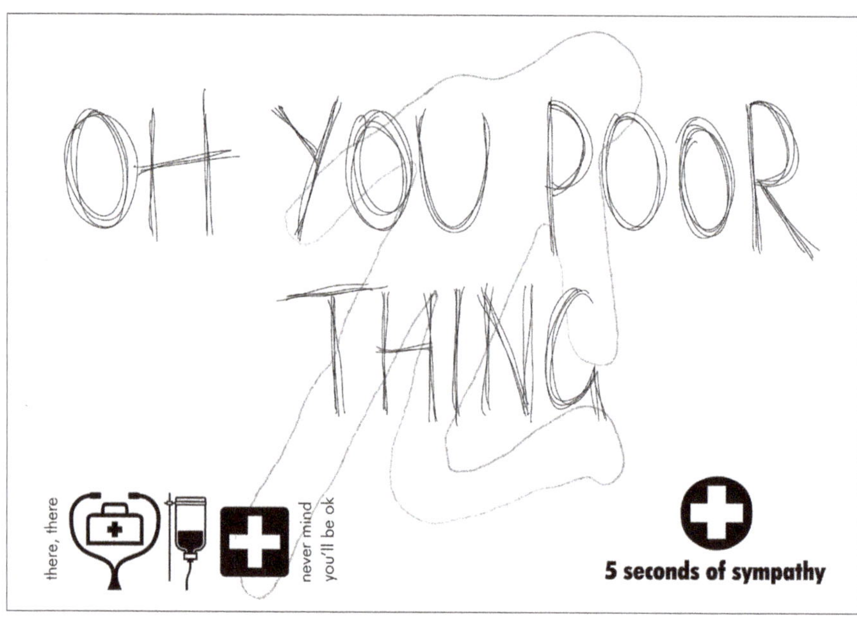

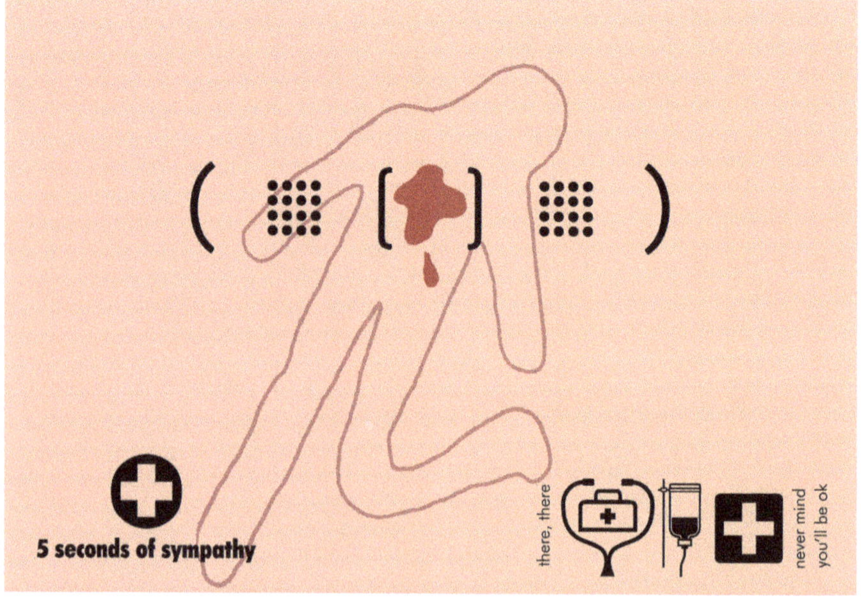

First appearances of the outline figure in 2006:
Oh You Poor Thing (top) and Bad Samaritan (bottom).

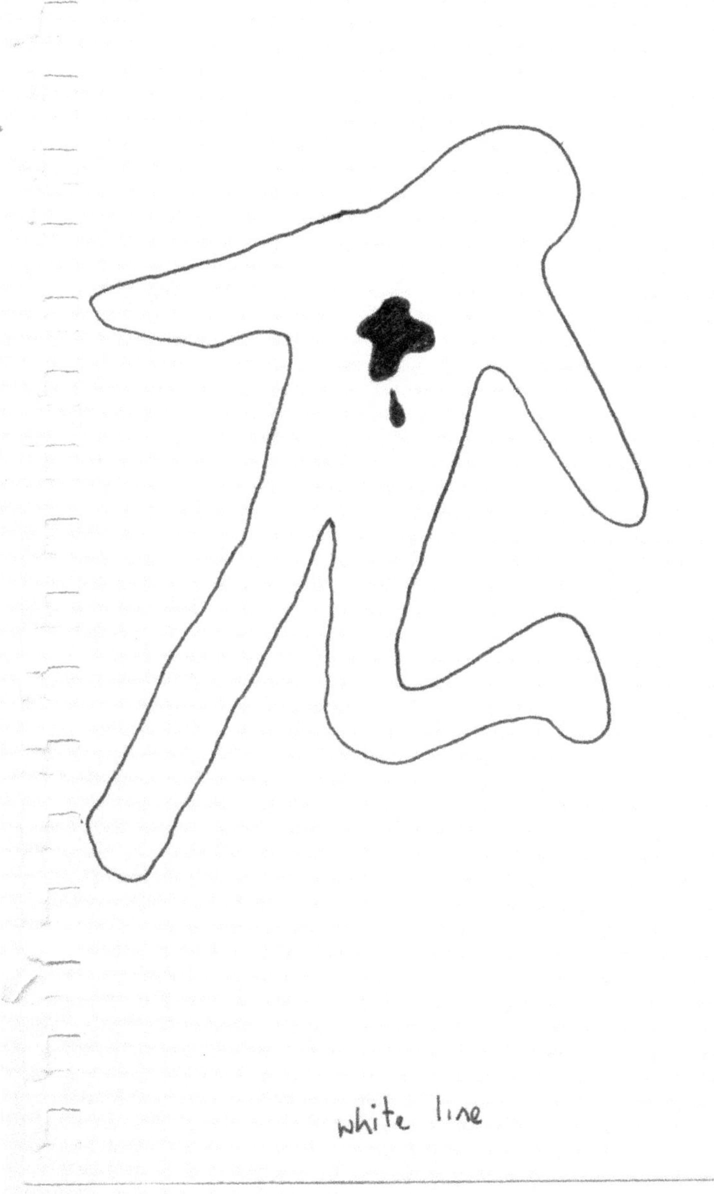

Notebook page: original drawing and scan
of the outline figure.

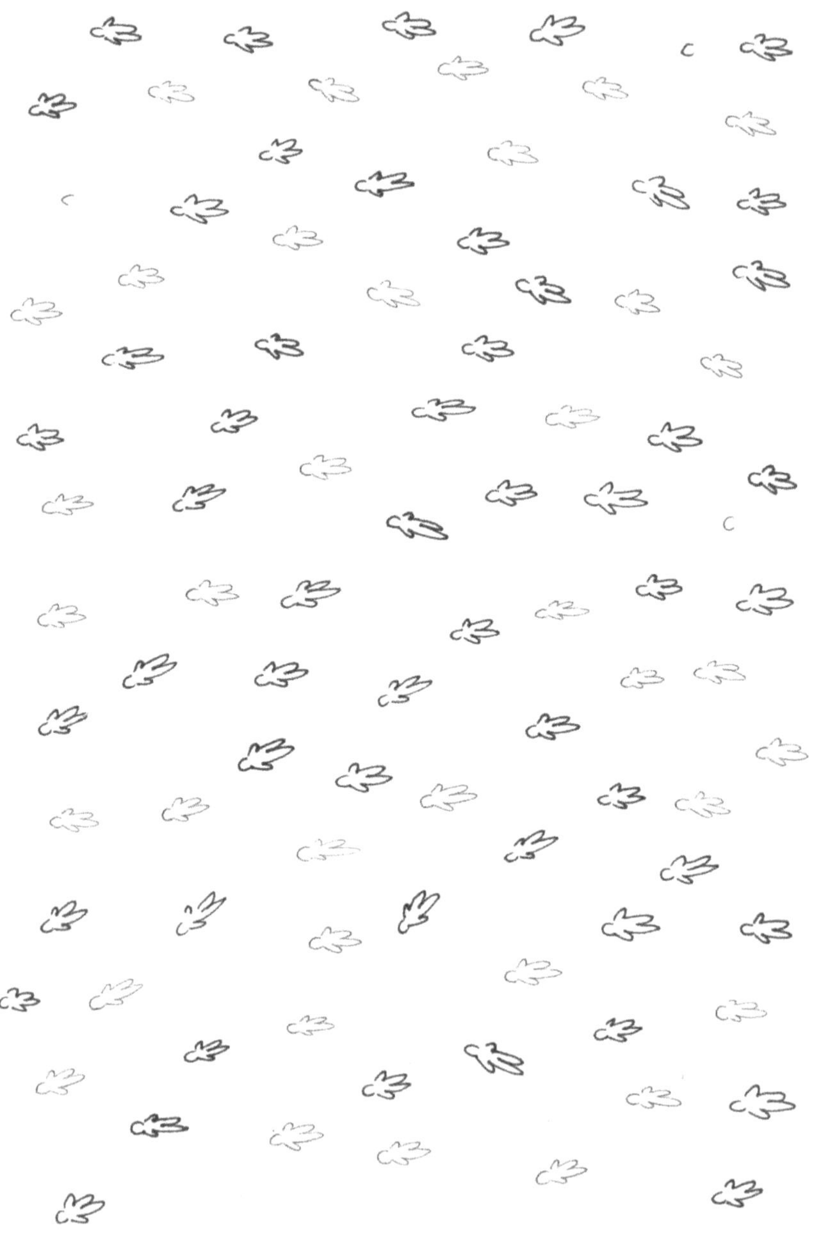

Cloud of witnesses: the original worksheet for
the hand-drawn Pride & Refuse figures.

Part Four:
Text

An Introduction (after the fact)

The Pride & Refuse project falls within the wider framework of
the Safe Little World concept, which deals with the paradoxes of
our internal and external worlds and spaces, the mundane and the
extraordinary.

It's an examination of the pitfalls, potentialities and aspirations of
humankind, and takes its title from an excerpt from *Pensées* (as seen
in the epigraph and prologue of this book) in which Blaise Pascal is
dealing with the paradox of what it means to be human. In its fuller
French context:

*Quelle chimère est-ce donc que l'homme? quelle nouveauté, quel monstre,
quel chaos, quel sujet de contradiction, quel prodige! Juge de toutes choses,
imbécile ver déterre, dépositaire du vrai, cloaque d'incertitude et d'erreur,
gloire et rebut de l'univers.*

Echoing Pascal, Rabbi Abraham Joshua Heschel expressed a similar
dichotomy: 'Man... is a duality of mysterious grandeur and pompous
aridity, / A vision of God and a mountain of dust.'

Meanwhile, 20th century American philosopher Dallas Willard
more gently fleshed out a related and relevant concept like this:
'The distance between the aspirations and the physical realities of
humanity can be the stuff of the ridiculous, the cynical, and the
tragic but at the same time be filled with compassion, faithfulness,
heroism, and creativity. In short, that distance is life as we know it.'

It's a big theme, but in this project it is handled with relatively simple,
small-scale visual elements and a sense of play that juxtapose with
the cerebral, metaphorical and existential scale of the main question.

Then comes a beautifully succinct reading, provided by Anna Sjardin-Killick (my wife): 'Pride & Refuse. We are the best and the worst of the earth. We fall down and we rise up.' And that's about all you need to know, unless...

—

The English version I originally used as the source of the Pascal quote, and therefore the title of this project, was translated by W.F. Trotter in the very early 1900s (later packaged with an introduction by T.S. Eliot). What's perhaps a little quirky about this translation is that the phrase *'gloire et rebut'* is translated as 'pride and refuse'. It would seem obvious to translate the phrase as 'glory and refuse'. Meanwhile, Google Translate renders *'rebut'* as 'scum', but Trotter's quirk stuck and happenstance results in my project's title being what it is, rather than Glory & Scum. Though my mate Dean Ellery reckons I might have sold more copies if the book had been called Glory & Scum.

—

Pascal introduces the flourish of his statement about humanity with the question, *'Quelle chimère est-ce donc que l'homme?'* Trotter renders this as, 'What a chimera is man!' Or in another version (Krailsheimer), 'What sort of freak then is man!' Pascal (more invitingly) frames the sentence as a question rather than a statement, and it rings similar to the biblical query, 'What is man, that thou shouldest magnify him?' (Job 7:17 KJV). Which, in turn, sounds even more impressive in the Latin of the Vulgate: *'Quid est homo, quia magnificas eum?'*

It's a concept that is, or could perhaps be, entangled with the theological notion of 'original sin' – i.e. the fall and essential 'fallenness' and/or 'badness' of humanity – a framework that

now brings me a little disquiet. But Pascal hasn't said that's all
we are – he's proposed a balanced appraisal, and it's probably an
existentially honest one as well. Humanity is clearly not always
what we're sometimes cracked up to be; not to mention our inherent
vulnerabilities and how many countless millions of us have ended
up on some form of trash pile over the millennia.

I'm also less fond of dualities these days. When a concept proposes
two poles, I now tend to look for (at least) a third term or position.
Where might Pascal's paradox, if it functions as a dialectic, take us?

In looking for the original source of the excerpt that forms the
prologue of this book, I came across some other interesting material
in the same blog post (once upon a time I liked to write in lowercase):

—

while researching [Christina Rossetti's] work [for my MA], i came
across a book [*Writing the Incommensurable*, Penn State University
Press, 1992] in which the author (mary finn) had critiqued
rossetti's poetry from the standpoint of a concept devised by søren
kierkegaard (the 19th century philosopher and theologian).

that concept was the idea of 'incommensurability'. i might be a little
patchy on this – i'm working from memory, and i doubt i ever fully
grasped exactly what kierkegaard was on about even at the time. but
for our purposes, and i'm probably hijacking kierkegaard's concept
here a bit, it describes in another way the tension described by
pascal in the quote above.

mary finn's point was that out of this tension – this struggle to unite
the paradoxes of the human condition – come some of the greatest
works of creativity.

kierkegaard overcomes this 'incommensurability' by something called 'the leap of faith' – i.e., while holding the paradox (in the form of 'doubt') to be evident and undeniable, the chasm can be crossed by making a leap of faith.

in the essay that resulted from my research (which also touched on the writing of [T.S.] eliot as well as rossetti) i argued that incommensurability was ultimately overcome [or rather, has the *potentiality* to be ultimately overcome] by 'consummation', i.e. the union of God and humankind (the Bible describes it in terms of Christ and his bride) that is ultimately furnished by God in the form of heaven, and (now that i think of it) the new heaven and new earth, and the kingdom of heaven, and the Word becoming flesh in Jesus.

—

That last phrase hits on it best, I think, from the perspective of Christian theology – Jesus Christ is the 'third term' for the paradox / duality / dialectic that Pascal observed.

But note how the tension – incommensurability, desire, longing – leads to creativity. And here we are.

I'm not sure if it happened in the same moment (the narrative of memory says it did) but as I lay there (on a pink recliner, though that's probably not important) reading Pascal under the blue sky as described in the prologue, I combined two disparate ideas… hand-drawn human outline figures (a motif I'd been thinking of for some time) with an interest that had been developing in the way of photographing skyscapes.

—

Part One of this book, the eponymous central piece (exhibited as
a 15-image cluster), visualises the paradox of Pascal's definition
of humanity through utilising the outlines of human figures
(originally aesthetically influenced by the chalk outline at a crime
scene) elevated, caught-up and floating in the 'heavenlies'. The
figures are found in community in the centre image but in solitude
in the surrounding images, exemplifying the human condition.

—

Most of the background images for this piece were photographed in
2011 with the westering sun in the vast skies over the Kaimai Ranges,
from the vantage point of the balcony of the house where we lived
in Brookfield, Tauranga, at that time.

These skyscapes became about the desire to see and capture
what I came to call 'lenticular fulgence', and about the dream of
being there; figures caught up, us, me, held and suspended there,
surrounded by the awe, the numinous silence, the harmony, the
glory. That's too much, but it's true.

A particular feel and desire, an aspiration, for the luminous
'diaphany' of the world (to use a word favoured by the French
philosopher and theologian Pierre Teilhard de Chardin).

—

Hi Mum

I don't know if you saw on Facebook a while ago, one day I posted
that I had two words stuck in my mind: 'lenticular' and 'fulgence'. I
put them together into 'lenticular fulgence' and said it out loud in
the kitchen as I was getting breakfast.

I might have heard the meanings before, but when they popped into my mind that day I didn't know the meanings consciously. When I looked them up, I saw that 'lenticular' is 'as pertaining to a lens' and 'fulgence' is radiance.

I really just posted it on Facebook as a curiosity, but I did start to wonder what it might mean... half jokingly, half with that old desire for meaning seeking to come to the surface.

First I defined the presence of the words as indicative of a desire to 'capture radiance'. I was thinking of 'lens' in terms of photography. The act of photographing is in part an act of appropriation – that is, taking what is out there and putting it in here. But of course a lens is also, in its basic meaning, a device that allows you to see. And often a particular lens will enable you to see in a way that you can't see otherwise. To pull it all together then: first of all to see the radiance, and then to capture it. This is artistically compelling, but flowing deeper still – it is spiritually compelling. To see radiance, to capture radiance, to appropriate radiance and to put it in here.

On my Facebook post, Arthur [Amon, friend and poet,] commented that the most common usage of 'lenticular' is in relation to cloud formations. And he deduced that my subconscious (or we could call it 'heart' or 'spirit') was seeking to find the 'silver lining on the cloud'. So this is also true... one interpretation of the possible meaning of 'lenticular fulgence' doesn't preclude the other. This morning I read in the Pilgrimage book [Andrew Jones, *Pilgrimage*, BRF, 2011], 'Timothy Radcliff sums this up well when he says that this is the kind of hope that means "daring to find ... eternity glancing through the clouds now".'

- Email sent to my mother (091113)

—

The Rapture (from the Latin *rapio*, meaning 'caught up') was a powerful image from the popular mythos of my childhood days. Described by St Paul in his first letter to the Thessalonians, within the pentecostal and charismatic environment I grew up in it was taken as a literal, specific 'end times' event that would occur on an imminent future date – 'any day now'. Christ would return in the clouds, and believers would ascend to meet him. You can appreciate the impact this might have had on my young imagination; and although I don't remember it being a conscious thought in the initial creative process for Pride & Refuse (I simply instinctively grouped the figures into community around a central, highlighted figure), it probably isn't surprising that an image like that appears to have made its way into a work about characters suspended in the sky.

The lonely figure is caught up, then finds his or herself in congregation... perhaps this is a time of rescue, an apocalypse, the commencement of a radical new epoch – an eschaton. Or perhaps simply a final flight at life's end. Quite apart from questions of literalism, the image, I think, speaks to the human condition, human longing, and sparks the imagination. All the great stories of humankind carry a type of archetypal grist.

—

I couldn't remember the exact wording, but a phrase I'd heard floated around in the vague archives of my mind. It had been used as a title by the writer Flannery O'Connor, taken from Teilhard de Chardin, and it was something like, 'All that rises must converge.'

I wasn't sure what it meant, or whether it was even true. But it seems my figures in rising are in the process of convergence, coalesced in the central image, around the central figure – maybe in some sense being drawn into that figure.

It transpires with further investigation that the conventional wording (and the title of O'Connor's short story) is 'Everything That Rises Must Converge', and the work by Teilhard de Chardin to which it refers is an essay called 'Omega Point' (the title of which, in turn, refers to the event when the universe spirals toward a final point of unification, the Logos, the Alpha-Omega, namely Christ, in whom all things hold together): 'Remain true to yourself, but move ever upward toward greater consciousness and greater love! At the summit you will find yourselves united with all those who, from every direction, have made the same ascent. For everything that rises must converge.'

—

Grand themes indeed. George MacDonald (C.S. Lewis's great literary hero) was a man gifted with the ability to turn an unexpected and magnificent turn of phrase. But in one of his less masterful couplets he says,

Thou mad'st the worm – to cast the wormy slough
And fly abroad – a glory flit and flee.

I assume he doesn't mean 'earthworm' (despite the presumably unintended pun regarding 'castings') or (as it sometimes is in literature) 'dragon', but rather 'caterpillar'. In any case, taken at face value, it paints a rather wonderful, if surreal, picture appropriate to our theme: of Pascal's *imbécile ver déterre*, the imbecile worm, rising up from muck and taking glorious flight. Just look at Mudwiggle go!

—

The counter-piece to Pride & Refuse (Part Two: Rising/Falling) is a sequence of nine images that tell the story of a hero's attempt at flight.

It was an act of play one day in the backyard in 2010, involving
flinging a cloth dummy into the air and photographing him,
which evolved into a narrative about escaping natural / physical /
metaphorical confines and limitations – whether that be the desire
to fly, a leap of faith such as the one described by Kierkegaard (a
'double movement' that goes up towards God, but also comes back
down to earth), the desire of Icarus to exceed mere escape from his
containing island and reach the fiery sun, or simply *l'appel du vide*
(the call of the void, the irrational urge to jump from a height). It
all escalated quickly, from play to high concept (always with the
possibility that it would descend again under the weight of gravity).

Perhaps we should just let the lad fly, and let him have his fun.

—

'One of [Kierkegaard's] most famous metaphors is the "leap of faith"
(actually Kierkegaard does not use this phrase, but he uses the
metaphor of a dancer's leap to illustrate the movement of religious
faith),' writes philosophy professor Clare Carlisle. 'This metaphor
expresses the way in which faith is a "double movement": it goes up
towards God, but it also comes down to earth, and this shows that
faith is not a withdrawal from the world but a way of living in the
world through a relationship to God.'

The philosopher and theologian Richard Rohr writes, 'Philosophies
and religions are either Ascenders, pointing us *upward* (toward the
One, the Eternal, and towards Absolutes), or they are Descenders,
pointing us *downward* (towards the many, the momentary, and
towards the earth)...'

In a Rohr-like move that breaks down a duality, I say let's have both –
the dancer's leap that contains the paradox – sacramentally 'moving

back and forth from this groaning earth to the earth eschatologically redeemed, from the earth eschatologically redeemed to this groaning earth,' as Craig Keen frames it in theological terms (drawing on ideas from Orthodox priest and theologian Alexander Schmemann about a 'liturgy of ascension' and return).

Could the performative act of tossing a cloth dummy into the air be considered a kind of sacrament – something 'down to earth' that embodies a deep truth or intentionality?

Take it easy, my son, keep it simple. Take a load off and enjoy lying in the grass, the sunlight filtering through the trees.

—

Is it a dancer's leap held within the atmosphere of the divine, or is it simply a leap into the void, an infinite expanse of no-thing-ness?

In Yves Klein's famous *Le Saut dans le Vide* (*Leap into the Void*) action of 1960, the artist threw himself from a pillar at the entrance of a pavilion, and was photographically suspended in curvilinear form, floating out over the pavement below. 'Far from falling,' says the blurb on the Yves Klein website, 'the artist seems to take off... A man in full levitation between heaven and earth...'

The resulting black and white image appeared in a special four-page newspaper called *Dimanche 27 Novembre 1960, Le journal d'un seul jour* (*Sunday 27 November 1960, The Newspaper of a Single Day*) published by the artist (as artists are wont to do) and released to the Parisian public.

International aspirations to put a man in space were in the general consciousness, and the image was accompanied by the text:

Un homme dans l'espace! Le peintre de l'espace se jette dans le vide!... Le monochrome qui est aussi champion de judo, ceinture noire 4e dan, s'entraîne régulièrement à la lévitation dynamique ! (avec ou sans filet, au risque de sa vie)... Aujourd'hui le peintre de l'espace doit aller effectivement dans l'espace pour peindre, mais il doit y aller sans trucs, ni supercheries, ni non plus en avion, ni en parachute ou en fusée : il doit y aller par lui-même, avec une force individuelle autonome, en un mot, il doit être capable de léviter... Yves: «Je suis le peintre de l'espace. Je ne suis pas un peintre abstrait, mais au contraire un figuratif, et un réaliste. Soyons honnêtes, pour peindre l'espace, je me dois de me rendre sur place, dans cet espace même.»

Which translates as:

A man in space! The painter of space leaps into the void!... The monochrome man who is also champion of judo, black belt 4th dan, practises regularly dynamic levitation! (with or without a net, at the risk of his life)... Today the painter of space must, in fact, go into space to paint, but he must go there without trickery or deception, and not in an airplane, nor by parachute or in a rocket: he must go there on his own strength, using an autonomous individual force; in short, he must be capable of levitation... Yves: 'I am the painter of space. I am not an abstract painter but, on the contrary, a figurative artist, and a realist. Let us be honest, to paint space, I must be in position, I must be in space.'

The picture was, in actual fact, carefully choreographed by the 'mystic and mythmaker who beguiled his admirers with the prospect of transcending the material limitations of earthly life', and the final effect was achieved through the trickery of darkroom compositing: 'Klein's wife and friends were holding a tarpaulin to catch his falling body... On the day of, he jumped many times ... practising the arc of his body and testing different elements in the scene.'

In the event pictured in Rising/Falling, I let my dummy do the practising and falling work, handling those manoeuvres on my behalf. But I accompanied him on that journey by imagination – just as I have always done in my playing since childhood… in the air with the kite, underwater with the stone, in a miniaturised environment with my Star Wars figures… the ability to let imagination transpose perception in concert with the action of play, and thereby lend a form of experience, an exploration, that flows from a desire to see, to be, to know, until such time as we can actually rise up in the sky, plunge beneath the surface of the water, inhabit new worlds.

—

In exhibition form, both pieces (Parts One and Two) were supported by a mobile of 15 cloth dolls or dummies (each about 25 centimetres tall) gathered in a cloud, while on the floor were a cluster of black vinyl adhesive outlines representing each of the figures in the Pride & Refuse photographs, at a scale similar to the suspended dummies.

The vinyl adhesive outlines were printed for free by the generosity of an Auckland printing company.

My father-in-law, René Sjardin, was the craftsman for the manufacture of the dummies. I went round to visit and see the process in action, to find that the original dummy (the hero of the Rising/Falling photographs) had 'laid down his life for his friends', becoming the pattern for the manufacture of the 15 new ones. It was a forlorn and poignant sight. The sort of thing that might make a polymath pensive.

Looking for a cheap source of materials, René stuffed the dummies with fill from pillows purchased at an op shop. Who knows what heads had rested there and what dreams those pillows had hosted. The cloud-like fibre now embodied as internal substance in the suspended dummies, floating above the gallery floor, containing the psychic residue of the oneiric journeys of unknown sleepers.

—

The Pride & Refuse installation has been exhibited twice.

The first occasion was at Transitions – an event hosted by the Lower Bar Collective between 31 October and 2 November 2014, combining sonic experimentation and art installations within the unique interior of the Silo 6 exhibition space in Auckland's Wynyard Quarter (a large cluster of concrete silo cylinders once used to hold powdered cement).

The dummies were hung from an in situ hopper, the vinyl outline figures adhered to the floor, and the Pride & Refuse and Rising/ Falling images hung on the rough walls as little framed 6×4 inch prints in two clusters.

I actually never saw this installation with my own eyes. On the weekend of the Transitions event, my wife's ill health prevented me from travelling up to Auckland. The elements were urgently shipped north, and my Lower Bar Collective compadres – in particular Mal Dunn – undertook the installation on my behalf.

The second exhibition was in a smaller, more conventional gallery setting – a corner of Zeus Gallery in Tauranga – for two weeks in November 2015. On this occasion, my mate Dean assisted me in the installation. So the piece took on significant indebtedness to a community of people.

A short video of this second installation can be viewed by visiting vimeo.com/144949315 or scanning the QR code below with your phone.

In this book, though the images are similar in size to their original 6×4 exhibited format, they appear (without frames) in linear form rather than cluster. This means they will tend to 'read' consecutively, rather than as a field or group. That changes the viewing experience (feel free to flick back and forth at random from page to page).

For Part One: Pride & Refuse, I have placed the centre image of the cluster in the middle of the series to echo its position in the exhibition hanging, rather than as the final frame, where it may have appeared as a narrative climax.

The more ordered original hanging format of Part Two: Rising/ Falling always suggested a left to right, top to bottom reading order (like the narrative sequence of a comic strip), so that group appears in the book accordingly.

I have included a layout schema for each cluster, to give an idea of the exhibition format, and the Silo 6 and Zeus installations are documented in Part Three.

The images from Pride & Refuse were also used as a video backdrop for the Lower Bar Collective musical piece, 'Ends in Tears'. You can

hear this track by visiting soundcloud.com/lower-bar-collective/
ends-in-tears or scanning the QR code below with your phone.
Serving suggestion: look at this book while listening to the track.

—

As you may have noticed, aspects of the Pride & Refuse project
became quite theologically engaged as I processed it conceptually –
it was always there in Pascal's original *pensée* (he was a man
fascinated by theological propositions), but the paradox of the
human condition and motifs of rising and falling, ascending and
descending, are so prevalent in Christian thought that virtually all
the most compelling ideas I came across that seemed to relate to
this project came from those kinds of sources. Theology is, at heart,
very often about the aspirations of humanity towards the divine –
ontologically, existentially, cognitively and imaginatively. It covers
a vast scope of what it means to be human, and so no thoroughgoing
description of the human condition is complete without it.

A theological framework is just another way to view the work, or
any work. I hope no philosophical prejudice forms between the
viewer and the work by those connections – I know the wide, deep
and diverse phenomenon reductively known as 'Christianity' carries
pre-existing baggage for individuals, but I hope the project can be
engaged on its own terms and the accompanying material viewed as
conceptually interesting, if nothing more. None of it is intended to

be didactic, and I hope the material gets pulled in all directions by
the viewer.

—

The other thing to know (which, again, may not have escaped the
reader's attention) is that the longer one of my projects sits around
(and they have been known to sit around for quite a while), the more
time I have to analyse them, to make meaning out of dreams.

And so the danger (if it is a danger) is that what might have
otherwise been simple, ephemeral, passing images (in this case, the
photo(graphics)) become weightier (or weighed down) with words.
This project is probably a bit like that. But what's done is done.

I have this urge to enclose my projects, and all the thought-
ephemera that goes with them, between covers. Even if no one reads
what's written. But I still consider the images to be the main event,
which is why I've placed my loose essay as secondary in this book.

You have utter permission (if it's not too late) to discard and go
off on a meaning-making journey of your own, to make your own
constellation of connections. There is a lot of verbiage here but
there's no way it's all the verbiage. And all the words in the world
can't be allowed, first of all, to preclude the possibility of a wordless/
unworded response. Each one of us is a universe full of experience,
pitfalls, potentialities and aspirations, pride and refuse, concept
and meaning(-making) – of our own dreams, and thoughts about
dreams. *Being* grounded and taking flight.

—

Suspended I
Floating I
Caught up I
We find ourselves
The community of all
At once dirt
And the breath of God.

Where my feet fall
Is ground
Of being
Pushed upward.
Animated.
Living and moving
In glory and
Pure air.

A Constellation of Connections

Have fun with the dot-to-dot puzzle on the opposite page. It's based on the central image from Part One: Pride & Refuse. See if you can join the dots, making connections in a wonderful constellation. There are no wrong answers, you can use as many lines as you like, straight lines, squiggly lines (or maybe even form a spiral) and any order is great. Below is one we created earlier in which every dot is linked to every other dot...

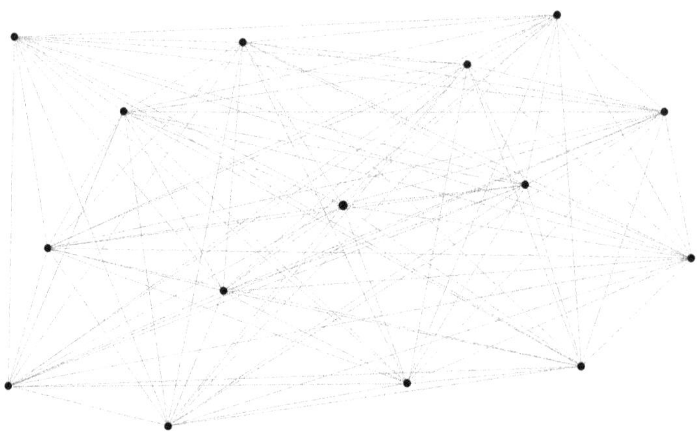

Pride & Refuse dot-to-dot puzzle.

Thoughts & Aspirations (A commonplace)

[William] Blake must have believed that every human being has
access to ... metaphorical aerodynamics; he drew figures depicting
the dramas of human existence, people flying, falling, coming to
earth or spiralling upward.

- David Whyte, Crossing the Unknown Sea

—

Kierkegaard ... uses both characters and metaphors to show the
movements of existence. One of his most famous metaphors is the
'leap of faith' (actually Kierkegaard does not use this phrase, but he
uses the metaphor of a dancer's leap to illustrate the movement of
religious faith). This metaphor expresses the way in which faith
is a 'double movement': it goes up towards God, but it also comes
down to earth, and this shows that faith is not a withdrawal from
the world but a way of living in the world through a relationship to
God. Abraham's journey to Mount Moriah provides another dynamic
metaphor for faith, and in fact this resembles the 'double movement'
of the dancer's leap because Abraham walks up the mountain and
then comes down again, returning to his home and to his wife Sarah.

[...]

Faith requires a leap because it holds together the contradictory
opposites of eternity and temporality, infinity and finitude, God and
the world.

[...]

Kierkegaard suggests that the 'boundary zone' between the ethical and religious spheres is humour. Whilst moving from the aesthetic to the ethical involves taking oneself *more* seriously, moving from the ethical to the religious involves taking oneself *less* seriously. The ethical individual – perhaps when she is close to despair – might suddenly see the funny side of her absurd struggle to live a completely upright life. She is striving with utmost determination for something that is impossible to attain! She might even laugh at her own seriousness, which is, in the bigger scheme of things, quite ridiculous. Humour arises from the insight that human existence is at once unbearably heavy and ultra-light; full of significance, and yet pretty insignificant; overwhelmingly difficult and very, very easy. Humour is transitional because, like irony, it brings a complete shift in perspective, and helps people to see themselves differently.

- Clare Carlisle, *Kierkegaard*

—

...at any given time there are more than a million people in the air...

- PBS video on airline data

—

['The Pulley'] is a concretising title, evoking a ... mechanism ... in the double bucket system used by builders lowering rubble from the top of a house, the descent of the full bucket on one side of the pulley raising the empty bucket on the other side, to be filled in its turn... In Herbert's poem, paradoxically, man is weighed down by his many blessings, which drag him away from God. The empty bucket of restlessness, ever dancing in the air, 'tosses' mankind up to God's breast. A commonplace artisan's tool is made to epitomise a central Herbertian theme – that suffering brings man to God.

- Ann Pasternak Slater, *George Herbert*

—

Gormley's larger and more significant project ... is to transform this building [the Old Jail in Charleston] into a series of spaces that in their different ways interrogate the dialectic of freedom and containment inherent in any attempt to inhabit a place...
A moment's consideration raises ambiguity as to whether they [the figures in 'Learning to Think'] are falling or rising. The bodies have either just left the room, or just about to enter, or are somehow suspended between this room and another. In any case they are no longer contained by the room; its boundaries have been transgressed, perhaps in an aspiration to escape, to freedom, perhaps in a desire to return, to belong again... [the work] points to the general truth that freedom and containment are each other's necessary condition; that the places we inhabit make concrete the values and aspirations with which each of us most powerfully identifies as a person.

- Richard Noble, 'The Utopian Body'

—

Our existence seesaws between animality and divinity, between that which is more and that which is less than humanity: below is evanescence, futility, and above is the open door of the divine exchequer where we lay up the sterling coin of piety and spirit, the immortal remains of our dying lives.

We are constantly in the mills of death, but we are also the
contemporaries of God.

- Abraham Joshua Heschel, 'Seesawing'

—

I have been shown the authentic bad news about myself, in a
perspective which is so different from the tight focus of my
desperation that it is good news in itself; I have been shown that
though I may see myself in the grim optics of sorrow and self-
dislike, I am being seen all the while, if I can bring myself to
believe it, with a generosity wider than oceans. I've been gently
and implacably reminded of how little I know a whole truth about
myself. I've been made unfamiliar to myself, and therefore hopeful;
I've had the grip of desperation loosened. Desperation may well
come back. In fact it may only feel as if desperation has slackened by
one infinitesimal notch, but it has slackened, it has eased, because
just for now I have been enabled to feel beyond it, or rather to
participate a little bit in the freedom of a feeling that flows beyond,
behind, beneath, around it. This is comfort, but it is not comfortable.
It is awkward, undignified, exposed, risky-feeling. It is like finding
that there is something in the thin air to lean on, something in the
void – something *about* the void – which will hold you up, but only if
you tip yourself madly onto it and ask it to take your weight.

- Francis Spufford, *Unapologetic*

—

...according to Gregory [of Nyssa] time and space, like all created
order, are diastemic (have extension) and thus are not permanent.

There is no extension in the Creator for in Him there is no interval or sequence. Time for humans is a stepping stone towards infinity and eventually must be overcome. Gregory both laments extension for the way in which it limits us and praises it for being the means by which we ascend into life with God (theosis).

- Andrew Kaethler, 'Re-Approaching Gregory of Nyssa'

—

To ascend is to rise, to be transformed or transfigured, to be, as it were, pulled out of one's self, to be turned inside out, to be divinised by God. Most religions have some type of ascension story as part of the legend of one of its heroes.

- Mark G. Boyer, Nature Spirituality

—

It has always been one of the deepest desires of the human heart to fly over the horizon, up out of the containment and boundaries that normal human living seems to impose.

- John O'Donohue, The Four Elements

—

Death, like high faith, levelling, lifteth all.

- George MacDonald, Diary of an Old Soul

—

Then shall the fall further the flight in me.

- George Herbert, 'Easter Wings'

—

Possibly the last take-off of all is something like that. When the time finally comes, you're scared stiff to be sure, but maybe by then you're just as glad to leave the whole show behind and get going. In a matter of moments, everything that seemed to matter stops mattering. The slow climb is all there is. The stillness. The clouds. Then the miracle of flight as from fathom upon fathom down you surface suddenly into open sky. The dazzling sun.

- Frederick Buechner, *Whistling in the Dark*

—

The very first pulsation of the spiritual life, when we rightly apprehend its significance, is the indication that the division between the Spirit and its object has vanished, that the ideal has become real, that the finite has reached its goal and become suffused with the presence and life of the Infinite.

- John Caird, *An Introduction to the Philosophy of Religion*

—

It is true indeed that the religious life is progressive; but understood in the light of the foregoing idea, religious progress is not progress TOWARDS, but WITHIN the sphere of the Infinite.

- William James, *The Varieties of Religious Experience*

—

You see, I want a lot.
Maybe I want it all:
the darkness of each endless fall,
the shimmering light of each ascent.

- Rainer Maria Rilke, *Book of Hours*

Sources & Acknowledgements

Judge of all things... Blaise Pascal, *Pensées*, VII:434, gutenberg.org/files/18269/18269-h/18269-h.htm, accessed 250521.

there's a quote that always nags around... andrewkillick.blogspot.com/2010/07/, accessed 070322.

Quelle chimère est-ce donc que l'homme?... archive.org/stream/lespenses00pasc/lespenses00pasc_djvu.txt, accessed 070322.

Man... is a duality of mysterious grandeur... Abraham Joshua Heschel, from 'Dust and Image', *I Asked for Wonder*, Crossroad Publishing, 2020 (1983), p74.

The distance between the aspirations and the physical realities of humanity... Dallas Willard, *The Spirit of the Disciplines*, HarperCollins, 1991, p46.

What sort of freak then is man! Blaise Pascal, *Pensées*, A.J. Krailsheimer (trans), Penguin Books, 1995, p34.

while researching [Christina Rossetti's] work... andrewkillick.blogspot.com/2010/07/, accessed 070322.

Remain true to yourself... en.wikipedia.org/wiki/Everything_That_Rises_Must_Converge, accessed 180422.

Thou mad'st the worm... George MacDonald, 'December 14', *Diary of an Old Soul*, public domain, 1880, Pinnacle Press, p122.

One of [Kierkegaard's] most famous metaphors... Clare Carlisle, *Kierkegaard: A guide for the perplexed*, Bloomsbury Academic, an imprint of Bloomsbury Publishing PLC, 2006, p122. © Clare Carlisle. Used by permission of the publisher.

Philosophies and religions are either Ascenders... Richard Rohr, 'Ascending and Descending Religions', *The Mendicant*, Vol 8, No 3, 2018, p1, cac.org/wp-content/uploads/2018/08/theMendicant_Vol8No3.pdf, accessed 120522.

moving back and forth from this groaning earth... Craig Keen, *After Crucifixion: The Promise of Theology*, Cascade Books, 2013, Kindle, loc1457.

a 'liturgy of ascension' and return... Alexander Schmemann, *For the Life of the World*, St Vladimir's Seminary Press, 2018, p37.

Un homme dans l'espace! Text and translation taken from yvesklein.com/fr/oeuvres/view/643/leap-into-the-void/, accessed 180422.

mystic and a mythmaker who beguiled his admirers... Mia Fineman quoted in an article, which also includes other text in this paragraph, at artsy.net/article/artsy-editorial-yves-klein-tricked-iconic-photograph, accessed 180422.

[William] Blake must have believed... David Whyte, *Crossing the Unknown Sea: Work as a Pilgrimage of Identity*, Riverhead Books, 2001, p7. © 2001 David Whyte, reprinted with permission from Many Rivers Press, Langley, WA, www.davidwhyte.com.

Kierkegaard also uses both characters and metaphors... Clare Carlisle, *Kierkegaard: A guide for the perplexed*, Bloomsbury Academic, an imprint of Bloomsbury Publishing PLC, 2006, pp41, 122, 83. © Clare Carlisle. Used by permission of the publisher.

at any given time... PBS video on YouTube (pre-Covid) about information data and airports, no longer available.

['The Pulley'] is a concretising title... Ann Pasternak Slater, Introduction, *George Herbert: The Complete English Works*, Everyman's Library, an imprint of the Knopf Doubleday Publishing Group, a division of Penguin Random House LLC, 1995, pxxxvi. All rights reserved, used by permission of the publisher.

Gormley's larger and more significant project... Richard Noble, 'The Utopian Body' in *Antony Gormley*, SteidlMACK, 2007, p28.

Our existence seesaws between animality and divinity... Abraham Joshua Heschel, 'Seesawing', *I Asked for Wonder*, Crossroad Publishing, 2020 (1983), p75.

I have been shown the authentic bad news about myself... Francis Spufford, *Unapologetic*, Faber & Faber, 2012, pp64-65. Used by permission of the author.

...according to Gregory [of Nyssa]... Andrew Kaethler 'Review: Re-Approaching Gregory of Nyssa', transpositions.co.uk/review-re-approaching-gregory-of-nyssa/, accessed 250422.

To ascend is to rise... Mark G. Boyer, *Nature Spirituality: Praying with Wind, Water, Earth and Fire*, Resource Publications, 2013, p115. Used by permission of the author.

It has always been one of the deepest desires of the human heart... John O'Donohue, *The Four Elements*, Transworld Ireland, 2010, p35.

Death, like high faith... George MacDonald, 'January 4', *Diary of an Old Soul*, public domain, 1880, Pinnacle Press, p10.

Then shall the fall... George Herbert, 'Easter Wings', *The Complete English Works*, public domain, Everyman's Library, 1995, p40.

Possibly the last take-off of all... Frederick Buechner, *Whistling in the Dark*, Harper San Francisco, 1993, p42.

The very first pulsation of the spiritual life... John Caird, *An Introduction to the Philosophy of Religion*, quoted in Henry James, *The Varieties of Religious Experience*, Duke Classics, 2012, Kindle, loc6354.

It is true indeed that the religious life is progressive... Henry James, *The Varieties of Religious Experience*, Duke Classics, 2012, Kindle, loc6354.

You see, I want a lot... Rainer Maria Rilke, from I,14, *Book of Hours*, Anita Barrows and Joanna Macy (trans), Riverhead Books, 2005, p71.

The quotes in this book have been included in good faith and with an eye towards fair use. Explicit permissions have been obtained where feasible. Some works are in the public domain. Rights holders may contact the author regarding any concerns through the avenues noted at the end of the book. If you, the reader, like the sound of any of the quotes, please support those authors by purchasing their books.

—

Thanks to: The Lower Bar Collective – in particular Mal Dunn for hanging the installation in the Silos. Elliot Mason at the late great Zeus Gallery. René and Lesley Sjardin for their support, and René for using his formidable sewing skills in crafting the exhibited cloth dummies. Benefitz (especially Kent) for sponsoring and taking care of the printing of the vinyl outline figures. Francis Spufford and Mark G. Boyer for permission to quote from their books, and once again proving that authors (if you can reach them) are virtually always excellent and generous people who make the permission-seeking process something of a joy. Georgie Goater, Kristian Larsen, Paul Buckton and Dave Simpson for their permission to use the photographs documenting the Transitions installation at Silo 6. Kathryn Overall, Aaron More and Anna Sjardin-Killick for their on-going patronistic belief in my creative projects; that belief means so much to me. The board and staff of Vaughan Park Anglican Retreat Centre, where Anna and I spent the month of May 2021 on a residential scholarship, enabling me to work on this publication. Creative wise-mind, Peter Crothall, for taking the time to critique some of the images in this book many years ago and for his positive comments (even if he did think sunset photos were a bit naff). Dean Ellery once again for his friendship and his printing expertise at the Toi Ohomai Te Pūkenga Copy Centre in Tauranga. Anna Sjardin-Killick again – it's the dancer's leap for us. And to my family – thank you for your love and support.

Much love.

Safe Little World is the umbrella/background concept, moniker or creative handle for the (visual, conceptual, textual) creative output of Andrew Killick. To support, visit www.patreon.com/safelittleworld.

Shadow Press was established in 2005 with the vision of publishing innovative (theo)artistic/poetic books (poetry, visual art, experimental, philosophical, theological). Having published a collection of poetry called *Epilogue*, it languished until 2019 and the publishing of *Islands*, the first of the Safe Little World Monograph series. This is the fourth in that series.

If you would like to purchase a print of any of the images in this book, please get in contact.

For more, visit www.safelittleworld.com and www.shadowpress.co.nz